Sandstone Climbing in Cheshi.

By Alan Cameron-Duff and Peter Chadwick

First Edition 1998

Stone

Published by Stone Publishing and Design
25 Burnley Road East
Waterfoot Rossendale
Lancashire
BB49AG
01706-221557
E mail: stone@zen.co.uk

First published in 1998

Printed by Ashley Printers
25 Dickson Street Liverpool L3 7EB

A CIP Catalogue record for this book is available from the British Library
British Library Cataloguing in Publication Data

ISBN 0 9533500 0 2

Other forthcoming titles by Stone Publishing and Design

Yorkshire Gritstone Bouldering
available 1st September 1998

1999 British Climbing Diary
available late 1998

The idea for this guide came whilst co-authoring a Rock Fax guide to the Costa Blanca with Alan James. After all it had to be easier producing a guide to a local area where I had learned to climb than jetting off across Europe to another country with another language we could barely speak! Well it didn't turn out to be that simple, nothing ever is. It has taken over two years to produce the most comprehensive and complete guide to the area ever written. I hope that using the guide will provide you with as much enjoyment as we have had discovering the wealth of climbing, sometimes classic sometimes esoteric, which lies on our own doorstep.

Anyone who has undertaken a project such as this will be aware that the behind the scenes help is invaluable. We would like to thank the following people for their assistance:

Hugh Banner, Steve Bromley, Lew Brown, Pete Burden, Arnold Carsten, Mike Collins, Jim Hewson, Mark Hounsly, Heather Fawcett, Joe Healey, Ewan McCallum, Rick Newcombe, Ken Travis, Pete Trewin, Derek Walker, Harold Walmsley and Geoff Wilde.

The layout of this book was inspired by that found in Rockfax guides designed by Alan James and Mick Ryan. ©Rockfax 1998,1992. Their independent production of cutting edge guides has provided us all with an invaluable and accessible source of information on climbing areas worldwide. The topos in this book were originally based on templates supplied with permission from Alan James. ©Rockfax 1998,1995.

The rocks at Helsby have long been the playground of Merseyside climbers. Some of the great pioneers such as Menlove Edwards, Colin Kirkus, A.B.Hargreaves and others practiced here. When the Wayfarers' Club published its small pocket guide in 1946, energetically assisted by the Liverpool University Mountaineering Club which cycled to Helsby on frequent Sundays, only obvious lines of ascent had been described. Frodsham and other outlying rocks in the Northwest had received little attention. Climbers had no hardware at their disposal, only a hemp rope and sometimes a sling or two for the protection of followers, not the leader! New generations of climbers have addressed themselves to numerous harder problems despite the encroaching vegetation. Almost every foot of Helsby now seems to have been explored, and the authors are to be congratulated for the monumental task of collating and pinpointing the profusion of new routes into a comprehensive guide, which is to be commended to beginners and tigers alike. They will find no shortage of interest here!

Arnold Carsten

Left: Arnold Carsten climbing Eliminate
1 E1 5b in 1946.
photo: Douglas Milner

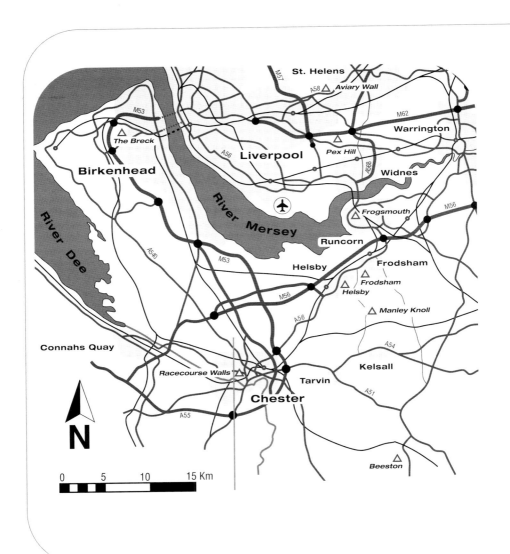

INTRODUCTION

CONTENTS

If it were not for the crags covered in this guide I would certainly have become a great man. As it was, all of my energy from a young age was directed to getting on and up these meaningless routes and problems. Taken under the wing and then led astray by a disgraceful cast of characters I was given little chance of redeeming myself and making anything of my life. Instead I broke bones, cut fingers, ripped tendons, lost girlfriends, signed on and dropped out. Oh, but what a great way to do it. The rocks covered by this guide offer some of the best bouldering in the country, along with some of the best routes in settings both beautiful and ugly.

The most impressive and neglected of the main outcrops is Helsby, often seen by motorists on their way to bigger things in Wales. Luminous green; it offers everything, blank walls, blank slabs, easy gullies, jamming cracks, well protected leads and classic solos.

Pex Hill, along with The Breck, provides some of the hardest, most technical bouldering in the country whilst Frodsham offers a desperate workout for the arms. The sport climber is catered for with Frogsmouth and the recently bolted Taylor Park.

A great many climbers visit the area, especially in the summer months; however the sandstone is quick drying in winter and Cheshire and Merseyside rarely receive the severe winters experienced on the Pennines and so stays popular.

However, what this area has above all others in England is a camaraderie rarely seen these days, summer evenings playing on the outcrops with a hundred unknown `friends' is not unusual on Cheshire and Merseyside Sandstone.

Pete Chadwick

HISTORY

When John Laycock published "Some Gritstone Climbs" in 1913 he recorded some twenty-five climbs at Helsby in his book. At that stage just seven routes merited the "severe" rating, among them the Overhanging Crack which was reckoned to be one of the hardest 'gritstone' climbs in England.

The mid-twenties saw considerable activity with members of the Climbers' Club, among them C.W. Marshall, producing a number of difficult and classic climbs such as Pigeonhole Wall, Hades Crack and, of course, Marshall's Climb itself. Another notable addition at this time was Wood's Climb, the work of the renowned Morley Wood, a member of the Rucksack Club. During the period 1928-29 the Wayfarers' Club put up twenty-three climbs, four of them led by F.E. Hicks but with the magnificent Colin Kirkus pioneering the other nineteen, including the still sensational Flake Crack.

This climb has undoubtedly claimed more lives than any other single route at Helsby, most notably that of C.W. Marshall himself who died of injuries sustained attempting the first solo early in 1928. Menlove Edwards, one of the most important figures in British climbing honed his legendary strength at Helsby where he achieved the first onsight lead of Flake Crack three years after Marshall's death. He had trained specifically for the ascent at the Adelphi Hotel gym in Liverpool! Kirkus, along with A.B.Hargreaves, went on to produce a guide for the crag published in the 1930 Wayfarers' Journal. Further developments, mainly by Kirkus, were recorded by R.C. Frost and F.G. Stangle in the Mountaineering Journal in 1935.

Prior to the next major phase of development which began in 1957 only a few climbs were added though the early post-war years saw Arnold Carsten publish his own guide which omitted several routes he considered unworthy, including that which now bears his name. It was only during the research for this book that "Menna" - his original name for what has for years been known as Carsten's Abortion - came to light. It was during the early fifties that Hugh Banner

started to visit the Helsby crags, producing Downes' Doddle (named posthumously after Bob Downes who had first noted the line but failed to lead it) and Twin Scoops amongst others. Another significant achievement around this time was the ascent of Quarry Buttress by John Evans. In 1957 Banner revised Carsten's 1946 guide and the 5c grade appeared for the first time.

The end of the decade saw the emergence, under the leadership of Banner, of the Helsby group which included a number of gifted climbers such as Ken Prandy and Jim O'Neill. This band climbed a number of hard and imaginative climbs matching anything that had so far been climbed on Gritstone, such as the cracks of The Mangler and Crumpet Crack and wall climbs like Brush Off and Brandenburg Wall. The hardest climb from this period was The Beatnik, so called because it beat The Sputnik at High Rocks in Kent; this was the work of Jim O'Neill who managed a toprope ascent and very nearly soloed it, only just living to tell the tale!

The Frodsham Buttresses were discovered around this time by the Helsby group. Jim O'Neill was especially active - e.g. Jimmy's Crack - but a quick look at the names of the routes indicates that some of the best climbers of the day also passed this way, as evidenced by Crew's Arete, Banner's Route and Boysen's Route.

During this decade John Victory, Jim O'Neill and friends started to peg and free climb their way up some of the loose walls at Frogsmouth which, despite their impressive size, deterred many visitors owing to the lack of protection and the friable nature of the rock.

The 1960s saw activity at Pex Hill with Rick Newcombe (in company with the Ashton brothers) climbing the wonderful Dateline one evening before rushing off to meet a young lady! The first guide appeared in 1965 and attracted a notable bunch to this superb quarry. Routes fell thick and fast to Ken Latham, Stu Thomas and others.

The same period saw another dank hole in the ground come alive. The preposterously talented Al Rouse started to use The Breck when he was fifteen and invited two seasoned climbers to come and try his routes; it transpired that neither Brian Molyneux nor Pete Minks could do any of them! In an attempt to get their own back they took him to the mountains of Wales, hoping to scare him on bigger and better things; they also got him drunk.
Rouse became adept in both disciplines! It should be noted that a number of lines at The Breck had already been climbed by Jim O'Neill.

Phil Davidson and the brothers Gaz and Joe Healey between them produced the hardest and best climbing in the Pex Hill quarry. These three skilful and competitive climbers dominated the local scene for over ten years. They produced such gems as Black Magic, Bermuda Triangle, Staminade and Monoblock. Like Banner and Rouse before them they transferred the techniques gained from the local area onto a wider stage and achieved some great ascents of the hardest routes of the day. Two characteristics made them shine - an effortless style and the ability to party like recently released lifers.

During the 1970s climbers from The Breck and Pex Hill would occasionally visit Frogsmouth and toprope a route or two which although undoubtedly hard were not recorded and attracted little interest. In the early eighties the super talented and highly trained Mike Collins, along with Lew Brown, climbed the classic Comet Crack, at the time a bold lead due to the dirt in the final section. It was during this decade that Parbold quarry was developed by local climber G.Harrison who together with S.Nicholson cleaned then climbed many of the routes on the Main Face. Tony Mawes, Les Ainsworth and laterley Ed Pearce continued to develop the venue adding most of the harder routes.

At Helsby, so thorough had the Helsby group of the late fifties been that activity slackened until the early eighties when the Pex and Breck mob turned their attention to the few remaining lines and "not leds". Phil Davidson soloed most of the latter with ease and

Mike Collins, Tom Jones and Joe Healey climbed The Runnells and 240 Volt Shocker amongst others. Due to the considerable efforts of John Codling and friends in the early nineties Frogsmouth was turned into an exciting and demanding sport climbing venue with the Big Stiff One really standing out!

Andy Griffiths, Mick Taylor and Tim Hatch brought Parbold screaming into the nineties with a free ascent of Ball Strangler the bold Too Loud a Solitude and the bolted Pit Funamentalist, the three hardest routes in the quarry. More bolts have since been added to the End Bay in an attempt to draw the crowds!

More recently Mike Collins, Pete Chadwick and Alan Cameron-Duff added some hard top rope problems to Helsby while Pete Trewin and Buzz Jones cleaned and climbed the few remaining lines at Pex Hill. Two local climbers (who wish to remain anonymous!) climbed over a fence, cleaned away the broken glass and bolted the neglected Aviary Quarry in Taylor Park to produce another slight but worthwhile venue. Recent hard climbing has concentrated on bouldering with the Frodsham crags receiving a thorough working by Ewan McCallum, Will Simm and Mike Collins details of these problems and many others at Pex Hill and the Breck have been recorded here for the first time.

Development has been so complete that last great problems are hard to find. However, Helsby has many Not Led's that await a bold and true first ascent and Frogsmouth has a number of blank spaces to work on. Frodsham, The Breck and Pex Hill will still yield many hard problems to the imaginative boulderer. Future crags await to be discovered, perhaps in the disused railway sidings and and abandoned cuttings of this industrial landscape.

In recent years the rock at a number of these venues has been abused, particularly at Pex Hill where Black Magic was horribly chipped. Let us hope that this trend has had its day and that the magnificent exploits of previous generations will inspire the climbers of the future.

Grades

A number of different grading systems are used in this guide. The English adjectival and technical grades, the French sport route grade and the American V bouldering grade.

English Adjectival Grade

For example, Difficult, HVS, E1 etc; this gives an overall picture of the route including how well protected and how sustained it is.

English Technical Grade

For example, 4b, 6b, 7a etc; this refers to the difficulty of the hardest single move.

French Sport Route Grade

For example, F6b F7b+; refers to the overall difficulty of the route without mentioning the difficulty of the hardest move. In this guide it has only been used for bolt protected routes.

American V Grade

The V grade originated in Hueco Tanks, Texas. It is an open ended system for grading boulder problems that takes into account the technical effort, power and stamina required to climb the problem. V grades start from V0 which roughly compares with English 5b, the hardest problems in the world at the moment are V14, which roughly compares with nothing at all in England on real rock! Confused yet? The following tables may help sort things out, then again it may not!

Protection

Climbing at the areas covered in this guide will require a variety of equipment:

Traditional Leading

At Helsby a full rack of gear is required to protect the climbs and provide adequte belays.

Bouldering Grades			
Hueco	Font	French (crag)	Eng (tech)
V0			5B
V1	6A		
V2	6A+		5C/6A
V3	6B	7A/7A+	
V4	6C	7B	6B
V5	6C+	7B+	
V6	7A	7C	6C
V7	7A+	7C+	
V8	7B	8A	6C/6C+
V9	7B+	8A+	
V10	7C	8B	7A
V11	7C+/8A	8B+	
V12	8A+	8C	7A+/7B
V13	8B		

French Grade	British Grade		
	Overall Diff.	Hardest Move	
Leading Grades			
2			
2+	D	4A	
3	VD		
3+	S		4B
4	HS		
4+		4C	
5	VS		
5+	HVS		5A
6a	E1	5B	
6a+	E2		
6b			5C
6b+	E3		
6c	E4	6A	
6c+			
7a	E5		
7a+			
7b			6B
7b+	E6		
7c			
7c+			
8a	E7+	6C	
8a+			
8b			7A

Take care when leading the rock can be dusty and very fragile! Some of the routes are in a very dirty, lichenous state, it is advised that climbs well within one's capabilities are tackled first. Remember most of the routes were toproped prior to a lead. Slings are useful for setting up top ropes as is a second rope for the same purpose.

Sport Routes

At Frogsmouth and Taylor Park the majority of the climbs need no more than a rack of quick draws and a rope. However a few use the odd wire or sling, so take a small selection of gear with you. Much of the gear at Frogsmouth is home made, bear this in mind when you are swinging about on it!

Bouldering

A mat and a rag for cleaning boots will help you in your quest for the difficult ascent, it will also leave a clean problem for the next climber who comes along. A soft tooth brush is useful for cleaning those micro crimps at The Breck and big slopers at Frodsham. Bouldering crash mats are useful for preventing broken bones and may well give the climber a few more years of use from their knees.

Environmental Conservation

Take care when climbing in this area and try to folow these guidelines, remember you are enjoying a fragile and limited resource.

Leading

Do not place bolts or pegs at crags where this is not the predominant ethic. Take care when placing protection in sandstone; a placement that fails will probably result in a damaged climb as well as a damaged climber.

Toproping

Do not have a rope running over the cliff edge, it is dangerous, expensive and will cause unnecessary erosion! Extend the belay with a sling or another rope.

Bouldering

Use only soft brushes to clean the rock. Clean the chalk off after your session as a build up is neither user-friendly or nice to look at.

Do not use resin! It will ruin the rock for other climbers.

Parking

Try to park considerately. Avoid damaging someone's pride and joy, be it their garden, car or child. When parking spread yourselves out, try not to cause congestion in one area.

Wildlife

Respect all wildlife. If a bird is nesting on or near your route, climb another route some distance away. See section on flora and fauna.

Access

Many of the crags in this guide are in areas frequented by the public so try and avoid any anti social behaviour which will cause offence to other users and may jeopardise future access for climbers. Further access information is given at the start of each section.

Symbols

P Shows where a peg is situated on the route.

 Lower Off. Indicates the end of a route and the means of descent.

 The walnut whip is awarded to a route of world class awfulness.

 Indicates a dangerous climb regardless of its grade. For example, an unprotected V Diff will be awarded a danger symbol over a reasonably protected E5.

NL The route has not yet been led.

★★ As with most guides, stars indicate quality, from one star indicating a good route to three stars indicating a fantastically stupendous route.

If a route is bolted this will be indicated in the route/crag description.

"O'Neill, responsible for so much of the development on the Frodsham Buttresses, rounded off a series of fine ascents by climbing the Beatnik: this route together with the Mangler is a standard harder than anything else on the crag and has necessitated the introduction of the grade 5d in this guide."
Martin Lee. A Climber's Guide to Helsby Crags

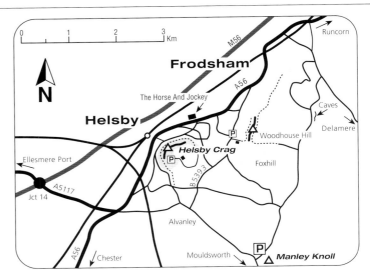

GENERAL

Before leading me away by the arm an old lady whom I had just met on the dance floor of a local night-spot said, "Well chuck, looks can be deceptive" and she was right! Helsby looks green and overgrown when viewed from the motorway below, however it is quite lovely and deserves to be climbed on more often. It has routes of great character ranging from 20 to 90 feet in length which often require a long neck. As a consequence of this many are toproped prior to a lead or solo. Don't let the complexity of arranging adequte top rope anchors put you off, many of the climbs are superb and are far more spectacular and exciting than their diminutive size would suggest.

ACCESS

The crag is owned by the National Trust. There are no problems with access to the main crag at the moment although peregrine falcons have been known to nest on the black buttresses of the upper tier. When nesting, an observation team keeps watch on top of the hill. **See notices for details of nesting restrictions from May to July.** The situation regarding access to Tennis Court Buttress is far more delicate, the right hand side of the Buttress is on private land and although the tennis courts are now overgrown and derelict it would be wise to keep a low profile or alternatively seek permisssion to climb. Similarly the land containing the quarries at the back of Helsby is also private.

INTRODUCTION

ASPECT

The crag receives the afternoon and evening sun and also gets a good drying wind from the Mersey estuary; consequently it is climbable all year round though routes on the eastern buttress can remain damp. The black upper tiers dry quickly after rain and are not affected by the thick coating of lichen which has caused problems on some climbs on the lower tier. The crag is extensive and complex which can lend some of the climbs a solitary feel; this is especially true of the less popular East Buttress.

APPROACH

The village of Helsby is on the A56 between Frodsham and Chester. The crag is clearly visible from this road and the M56. The best approach is from the base since parking at the top is currently a problem. Take any road from the village to the foot of the hill where a number of paths lead up through attractive woods to the crag. To park on top of the hill turn up Old Chester Road by the cemetery opposite Helsby High School. Take the first left and then first right; this road is a dead end and will deposit you near the top of the hill. There are only two or three parking spaces available in a layby at an obvious wood, so please be sensible and do not crowd. From the parking space continue walking up the road towards the farm, turn left down a short lane, then cross a stile on the right and walk to the top of the hill. Turn left and descend a steep path to the end of the West Buttress.

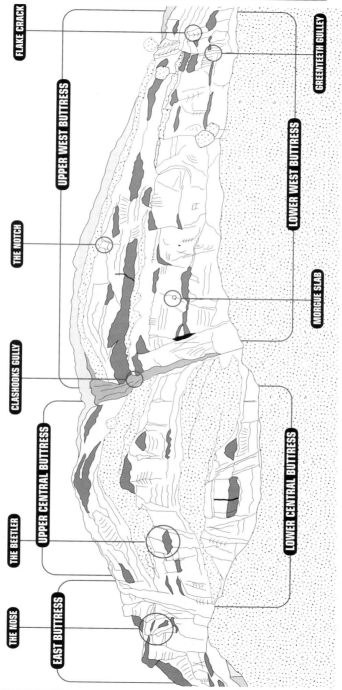

FLAKE CRACK

GREENTEETH GULLEY

UPPER WEST BUTTRESS

LOWER WEST BUTTRESS

THE NOTCH

MORGUE SLAB

CLASHOOKS GULLY

UPPER CENTRAL BUTTRESS

THE BEETLER

LOWER CENTRAL BUTTRESS

THE NOSE

EAST BUTTRESS

OVERALL VIEW

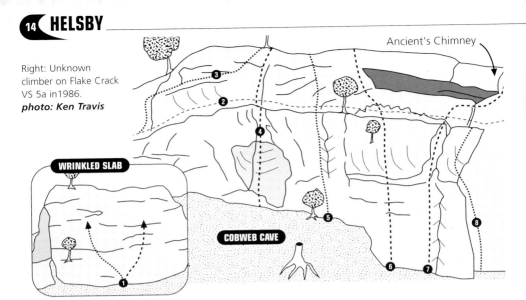

Right: Unknown
climber on Flake Crack
VS 5a in1986.
photo: Ken Travis

Ancient's Chimney

WRINKLED SLAB

COBWEB CAVE

Other crags on Helsby Hill
The woods on top of the hill contain a number of small vegetated quarries. Take the approach to the top of the hill and park in the layby next to the wood. Follow the path into the woods. The first quarry is an obvious pit about 25 feet deep with an impressive back wall. Further on is a large shallow quarry recognisable by a number of fine aretes and an 'attractive' curved bouldering wall. Most of the lines have been climbed, but the whole quarry would benefit from extensive gardening. There is another small quarry opposite the houses 100m up the hill just off the road which is partially filled with water and rubbish!

Helsby Crag
Behind the East Buttress there are some impressive overhangs lying on private farm land. They have been climbed on in the past but access is unclear. Below the summit trig point there is a small band of rock offering bouldering problems from Diff to 5b.

The Far East Buttress at the far left hand side of the crag offers some steep and imposing climbs with macabre names.

1   Wrinkled Slab M
The diminutive slab at the extreme left hand end of the crag. Crampons may be required due to the thick coating of lichen!

2   Halfway Ledge D
Climb/walk across the obvious ledge high up.

3   Far Eastern Traverse VD
Start on the eastern end of the Halfway Ledge. Climb up 10ft to the obvious traverse; follow this right.

4   Cobweb Cave Climb HVS 2,5b
Climb up the left edge of a small cave to the ledge, then up the thin crack above.

5   Torsion Crack VS 5a
Climb the crack right of the cave to the ledge, then the overhang and rounded slab above.

6   Millwall F.C. HVS 5b
Climb the centre of the bulging wall to the Halfway Ledge.

7   Jericho Wall HVS 5a,5b+
The thin vegetated crack to the right is climbed to the halfway ledge, followed by the interesting 'Ancient's Chimney' which takes the obvious gaping orifice above.

8   Philistine's Prowl VS 5a
The wall just to the right is taken without recourse to the crack on the left, finishing at the block on the Halfway Ledge.

FAR EAST BUTTRESS

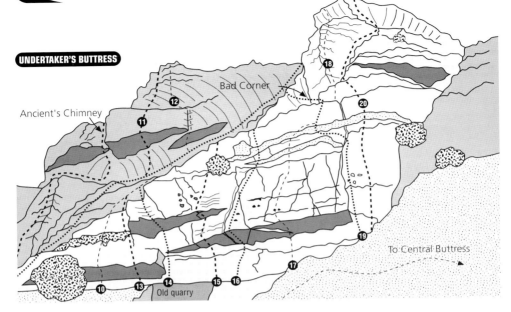

UNDERTAKER'S BUTTRESS

Bad Corner

Ancient's Chimney

To Central Buttress

Old quarry

9   Wall and Slab VD
The scoop to the right of the previous route is climbed until a traverse right allows access to the slab above.

10 Groove and Slab D
Climb the crack to the right starting from a grassy ledge, finishing by easy scrambling rightwards.

The next two routes climb the big overhanging wall above the rampline.

11 2001 NL 6c   ★★
Start up Groove and Slab. Climb into the corner then climb the bulging wall and roof above on black rugosities to finish up the left side of the prow. Scary and spectacular.

12 Space Odyssey NL 6b +   ★★
Start up Groove and Slab. Climb up a vague flake to the right of the previous route then over a bulge into a hanging corner, move left and climb directly over the hanging prow. Superb but fragile.

There is another line on the overhanging wall to the right which has yet to be climbed.

13 Quarry Buttress Direct HS 5a
Ascend the wall just left of the quarry then traverse right to finish up a V chimney.

14 Quarry Buttress Super Direct E2 5c
This superdirect version climbs directly above the quarry to reach the same chimney via a difficult groove.

A pointless route - Quarry Traverse - VD, crosses the top of the quarry.

15 Tyburn Wall E3 6a
Climb the overhang via an obvious flake just right of the quarry, to finish past a birch tree. Dubious rock.

16 Gallows E3 5c   ★★
10 feet to the right climb the pockets in the vague arete; an X marks the spot.

17 Lynch Mob Mentality E3 6b
A scary boulder problem, climb the roof and steep wall six feet right of the previous route via a pocket. Join the next route at about 20feet.

FAR EAST BUTTRESS

THE NOSE

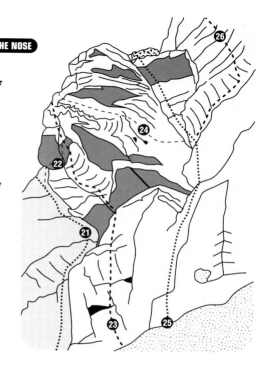

18 Night of The Living Dead NL 5c   *
The short but spectacular arete.

19 Corpse's Walk S
Climb the deep crack for 20ft then traverse left
until an escape can be made up to a finish just
left of Bad Corner.

20 Undertaker's Buttress S 4b   **
An impressive route up the big buttress. Climb
up the delicate wall just right of the crack of
Corpse's Walk, trending left to a ledge close to
Bad Corner (possible belay). Climb the crack
above to another ledge to finish up the short
steep black wall above. The original route
climbed the continuation crack of Corpse's Walk.

The short crack high up to the right is
The Drainpipe (M), a useful descent.

21 Stoic's Corner VD
The tricky corner at the right hand end of the
recess left of The Nose.

22 Upper Lip HVS 5b
Begin as for Stoic's Corner, then make a sneaky
traverse right to gain the final crack of Upper Lip
Direct. Finish up this.

23 Upper Lip Direct E3 5c
The severely undercut crack directly below the
final crack of Upper Lip.

24 The Nose VD   *
Climb up the chimney, then traverse out left
across the void to finish up a short crack. A
lower version, The Nose Direct, follows jugs
along the lip (5b).

25 Nose Gully VD
As for The Nose to the wide platform, then
ascend the left wall directly, turning the capstone on its left. Direct over the capstone is 5a.

26 Cinderella HVS 5b
Climb up to the obvious ledge as for Nose Gully
and ascend the short bulging black wall at the
centre of the bay on the right.

The next section of rock is known as Central
Buttress. The first part forms a big pillar the left
side of which is taken by the following three
routes. Further on the buttress is split into two
distinct tiers.

27 Omega VS 5a   *
20 feet right of The Nose. Traverse right along a
grassy shelf and up a short wall to a hand
traverse right to gain a ledge. Move up to a triangular stance on the right, then climb up left to
finish left of a small tree (This route is not shown
on any diagram).

THE NOSE

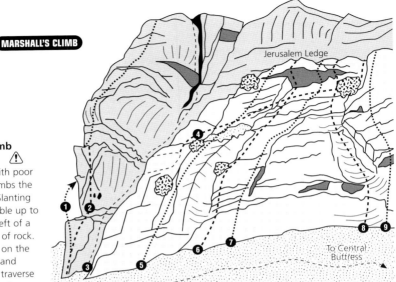

MARSHALL'S CLIMB

Jerusalem Ledge

To Central Buttress

**1   Marshall's Climb
HVS 4c ✶✶** ⚠
A good route with poor protection, it climbs the buttress left of Slanting Chimney. Scramble up to a ledge on the left of a square cut nose of rock. Climb the crack on the left of the nose and make a difficult traverse back right to a ledge on the crest, finishing up the slab above.

2   Marshall's Tower Eliminate E1 5b ✶✶
An excellent direct version of the original up the wall just right of the arete.

3   Slanting Chimney VD
Climb up the obvious chimney to a large ledge, Jerusalem Ledge. Choose any of the following lines to finish, between Mod and VD:
(a) The narrow chimney on the left.
(b) The wider slabby chimney
(c) The thin crack at the left hand side of the ledge.
(d) A strenuous rotten crack 15ft right.
(e) A short crack further right
(f) The groove in the slab to the right.

The following four routes all reach Jerusalem Ledge and use any of the finishes to Slanting Chimney detailed above.

4   The Traverse Route Mod
A poor wandering route. Follow Slanting Chimney until a long traverse can be made rightwards to gain the Lookout. From here climb leftwards up fangs of rock - the 'Golden Stairs' - to

Jerusalem Ledge. Finish up Slanting Chimney.

5   Coffin Buttress HS 5a
The small buttress 20 feet right of Slanting Chimney. Go via a left slanting crack, gain a ledge and continue up the buttress to Jerusalem Ledge.

6   Eliminate II VS 5a
Climb the obvious grass choked crack to Jerusalem Ledge.

7   Cemetery Wall HS 4b
The crack in the wall to the right.

8   The Coffin HS 4b
Climbs up the interesting 'coffin' feature to Jerusalem Ledge.

9   Tombstone Wall HVS 5b
The green wall 5 feet to the right of The Coffin.

The obvious green overhang of The Beetler dominates the next section of the cliff which is usually very dirty. A prominent flat topped block - The Lookout - can be seen high and left of The Beetler and is reached by the following two routes.

CENTRAL BUTTRESS

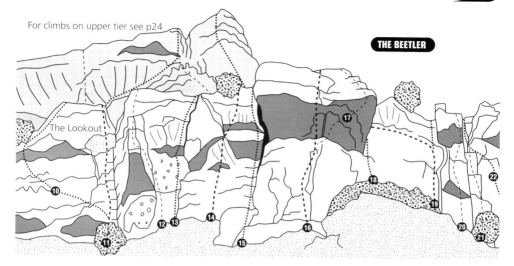

For climbs on upper tier see p24

THE BEETLER

The Lookout

10 Lookout Climb HS 4b   *

Start under the obvious corner and climb up
knobbly rock leftwards then back right to gain
the top of The Lookout.

11 Zig Zag Climb VD

Climb the obvious dirty corner to the right of
Lookout Climb to the ledge and finish up
Lookout Climb itself.

From The Lookout a variety of finishes can be
made up the steep black rock forming the upper
tier of the buttress, see page 24 for details.

12 The Thingummy VS 5a

Gain the ledge on Spider Crack from the left.
Move back left onto the prow then climb the
wall above to the top.

13 Spider Crack E1 5b

Takes the obvious crack through steep ground.

14 Greenshield NL 5c+

To the right of Spider Crack climb the wall and
roof with difficulty below a large tree.

15 Green Chimney S 4a

Climb the steep slab before entering the uninvit-
ing chimney just left of the Beetler overhang;
the scene of a near fatal epic for one of the
authors!

16 The Beetler E1 5b   ⚠

Climb the centre of the big slab and overhang on appalling rock.

17 Strength Through Joy NL 6b   *

Upon reaching the roof of The Beetler break out
right and climb the hanging arete in a silly position.

18 Sculptor's Climb HS 4b

Takes the slight, neglected corner just right of
the roof; the final mantle is the crux.

19 Chimney and Traverse S 4a   *

The steep cracked corner leads to a traverse left
to join the top of Sculptor's Climb; alternatively
finish direct.

20 Superdirect HS 4b

Climb the narrow crack six feet right of the
chimney to finish as for Central Climb.

21 Direct Route S 4a

Climb the overhanging niche to finish up
Central Climb.

22 Central Climb VD   *

Takes the wall to the right, then moves left onto
the rib to ascend easily to the top. See diagram
on next page.

CENTRAL BUTTRESS

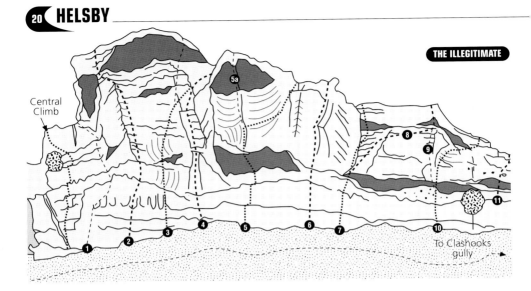

THE ILLEGITIMATE

Central
Climb

5a

8

9

11

10

To Clashooks
gully

To the right the wall steepens to form some impressive black aretes and roofs. Most of the climbs here are serious leads. Rare birds have in the past used this buttress for nesting. **If there is any indication of nesting in this area please climb elswhere!**

1 Easy Buttress D
Surprisingly the easiest way up this section of rock.

2 The Illegitimate E3 5c ★★★
Climb the spectacular arete and breach the roof at its narrowest point.

3 Brown's Bastard E2 5b
To the right of the previous route the over-hang is split by a slight weakness which is fol-lowed to join the parent route, Carsten's Abor-tion. The Forceps finish climbs directly over the final roof at 5c.

4 Carsten's Abortion E2 5b ★★
Tackle the steep twin cracks past the guano stained nesting site and exit right below the roof. Originally called Menna - the name of the first ascentionist's then girlfriend.

5 Downes' Doddle E2 5b ★
Gain the ledge in the scoop then teeter rightwards to a crack; climb this to finish on a disturbingly rocking block! A direct finish - Clockwork Orange - has been toproped at 5c, and involves powering up the overhang directly (No.5a).

6 Technicolour Yawn NL 6a ★★
A fingery and difficult problem up the small groove. Harder than it looks.

7 The Cornice VD ★★
A good climb. To the right of the last climb is a slanting corner capped by an overhang. Up and over!

8 The Cornice Indirect S
Traverse right and finish up Deception for an alternative finish.

9 Deception HVS 5a ★
Climb the small overhang and up the blunt arete.

10 Mossy Slab VD ★
A pleasant climb, paradoxically free of moss. Start as for Deception but pull across right onto a sloping slab, finish up this.

CENTRAL BUTTRESS

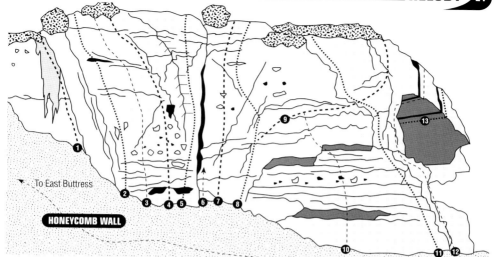

HONEYCOMB WALL

11 Gather No Moss E2 6b
A serious boulder problem up the faint scoops on the undercut wall to the right.

The tier below is composed of softer rock prone to becoming very dirty after bad weather. When they are clean some of the climbs are excellent.

1 Little Light S 4a
A New Brighton beach style crack!

2 Blue Light E1 5c
The left arete/wall.

3 In The Pie E1 6a
A hard eliminate up the wall to the right.

4 Pigeonhole Wall VS 5a *
A great little route on good rock.

5 Pigeonhole Arete E1 5c *
Between Pigeonhole Wall and Crack of Doom. A nice eliminate, Doom Wall (E2 6a) climbs the pocketed side wall between Pigeonhole Arete and Crack of Doom.

6 Crack of Doom VD
Deep and grubby. Jamming and bridging will help.

7 Whimper E1 5c
Whimper upwards utilising some small pockets on the wall to the right.

8 Wafer Wall E1 5b ** ⚠
Just right again, climb the wall using thin holds with little in the way of protection.

9 Z Route VD
More of a funny N than a Z. Move up diagonally to reach a rightwards traverse before crossing Oblique Crack and finish up the nose beyond.

10 Z Route Direct S 4a
Reach the middle of the traverse of the mother route from directly below.

11 Oblique Crack VD
The obvious but overgrown slanting crack.

12 Muffin Crack HVS 5b *
The left hand roof crack.

13 Crumpet Crack E3 6a ***
A classic struggle over the big roof.

CENTRAL BUTTRESS

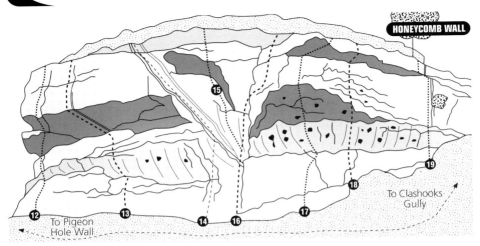

14 Hades Crack HS 4b
The crack just right of the prominent roof.
Steep and strenuous.

15 Wild Oat Wall HVS 5b
The tricky wall between the two cracks.

16 Two Step Crack VD
The right hand stepped crack.

17 Honeycomb Wall VS 4c *
Short but enjoyable climbing over the small roof
on big jugs.

18 Nameless Wall VS 5a
The pleasant wall to the right.

19 Nameless Crack S 4a
The thin crack at the right hand
end of the tier.

The following routes are on the
upper tier above The Beetler and
The Illegitimate. Refer to the plan
on the right.

**1 Grooved Wall Route 1
Direct Finish E1 5a** ⚠
Climb the fragile overhanging
wall above The Lookout.

**2 Grooved Wall Route 1
VS 4b** ★★
From the top of The Lookout climb into the
alcove on the right, then traverse right and climb
up the spectacularly positioned steep groove to
the top.

3 Grooved Wall Route 2 HS 4b *
Start 20 feet right of The Lookout, go up a short
corner and wall and then traverse left to join the
finish of the previous route.

4 Unknown E2 5b ⚠
Climb the right edge of the prow on doubt-
ful rock.

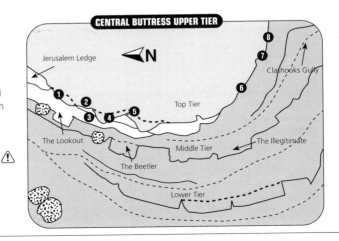

CENTRAL BUTTRESS

5 Fat Man's Crack VD
Further round to the right is a recess of rock, climb the crack at the back of the recess.

Further right a rounded slab and short steep black wall give the following routes.

6 Clashooks Slab M to HS
The small slab above the gorse bushes can be climbed almost anywhere. It tends to stay dry and clean because of the way it faces.

7 Limpet Wall HS 4b
The wall six foot right of the break; begin where "Scotland" is scratched in the rock.

8 Mussel Wall VS 4c
Climb directly up the steep black wall to the right. Two other routes have been recorded here, Crab's Crawl (VD) which traverses the stretch below the roof and Clashooks Traverse (VD) which traverses the entire wall.

The cliff is now split by Clashooks Gully. At the very top a short overhanging wall above the sand pit can be climbed in the centre at 5b or just to the right which is more strenuous at 5b+.

On the right of the Gully the cliff is split into two distinct tiers, the lower tier facing the Gully is broken and has few climbs of merit.

1 Celerity Crack HS 4b
Halfway along the lower section of West Wall is a good ledge which peters out into the gully. Just left of this is a bulging crack beginning at a height of eight feet. Climb this to Broad Walk.

2 West Wall Climb D
Gain the ledge of Celerity Crack by a hand traverse and climb the short crack to Broad Walk.

3 West Wall Mantleshelf S 4b ★
15 feet to the right of Celerity Crack mantleshelf into an obvious crack and climb it, avoiding the overhang by traversing rightwards.

4 The West Wall E1 5c
Gain the obvious curved flake by a difficult move from the left; continue up the flake, fighting your way onto the grassy ledge above.

5 Unknown NL 6b
Gain the faint curved crack by means of a long reach.

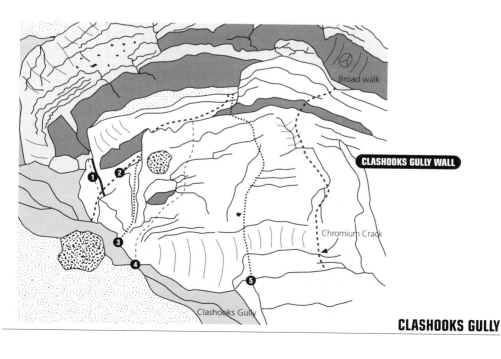

CLASHOOKS GULLY

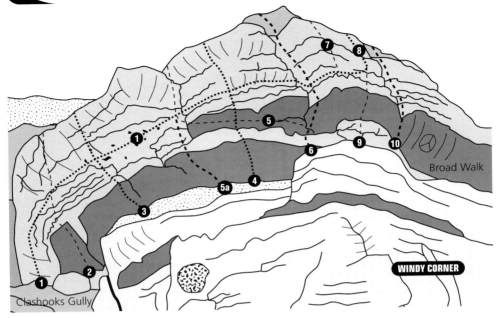

Broad Walk

WINDY CORNER

Clashooks Gully

The black overhangs on the tier above provide some exciting and impressive routes which are climbed from a large ledge - Broad Walk.

1   West Wall Traverse E2 5c   *
Traverse along the obvious break above the roofs from Clashooks to finish up Windy Corner. Wild!

2   Hemingway's Wall E3 5c   ** ⚠
Climb the overhanging wall above the boulder in the gully via a rounded shelf. Another start is possible 6ft right at 6a.

3   Late-nite Greenhalgh E3 6a   ** ⚠
Make difficult moves over the roof at a vague corner 6ft right and climb directly up the steep wall above.

4   The Missing Font NL 5c
Straight up 10ft left of the chimney via flakes in the roof.

5   Senile Saunter E1 5b   *
Climb West Wall Chimney until you can traverse 25ft left and climb the hanging corner crack to

the top. The corner can be also reached directly at 5c (No: 5a).

6   West Wall Chimney VD
Up the obvious chimney until it becomes too narrow when the left wall can be taken to the top.

7   Windy Corner Nose Finish HS 4b   *
Climb the previous route until a ledge on the right can be gained; traverse right a few feet then continue up the wall above to the top. Exciting!

8   Windy Corner VD
The original route continues the rightwards traverse, crossing Diopera and finishing round the face of the buttress until the route becomes a path, literally!

9   Unknown NL 5c
Climb the wall 6ft right of the chimney.

10   Diopera HVS 5a
Corkscrew up the weakness in the overhangs at the corner of the buttress.

UPPER WEST BUTTRESS

11 Eroica HVS 5a
Climb the strenuous overhang to the right on big fragile holds, finishing delicately up the wall above.

12 Erotica NL 6b
4ft right of Eroica. Climb out of a vague recess on shallow pockets and up the easier wall above. Poor rock.

Further along Broad Walk the overhangs get bigger and the routes get better.

13 Coward of the County E4 6a ✶
The crux is the bottom 10ft. Make a difficult move off the floor to reach a jug on the right, move back left and finish up the steep black wall above.

14 Spooky E5 6b ✶
Spooky! 12ft right use a small pocket and a long reach to gain good holds; move left and continue up the wall above.

15 Brandenburg Wall Direct NL 6b/c ✶ ⚠
Serious to lead, serious to toprope; don't fall off! Based around some small pockets from which a massive stretch is needed to gain a small prow. Finish up the flakes of Brandenburg Wall.

16 Brandenburg Wall E4 5c ✶✶✶
One of the best routes at Helsby. Hand traverse the lip of the roof, pull up and climb directly up the excellent wall.

17 Stingray E4 5c ✶✶✶
Climbs the wall above the start of Brandenburg Wall; where the parent route traverses left it continues direct using small flakes.

18 The Mangler E3 6a ✶✶
The classic roof crack. Jamming can be avoided if you have strong fingers; finish up the black wall. The roof to the right has been climbed without using the crack (Route 18a). Good but rather an eliminate at 6b.

19 Gorilla Wall E3 5c ✶
Traverse right along the obvious flake and climb the wall above.

20 Gorilla Wall Direct E4 5c ✶ ⚠
Climb direct up to the top wall of Gorilla Wall starting on big holds 8 feet right of the parent route.

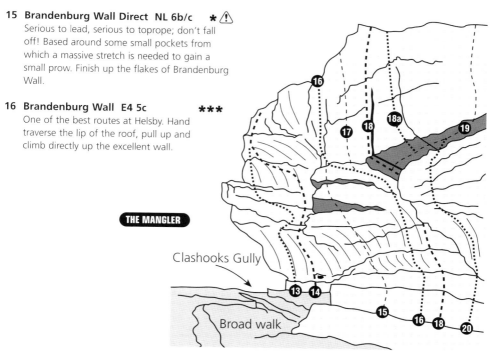

THE MANGLER

Clashooks Gully

Broad walk

UPPER WEST BUTTRESS

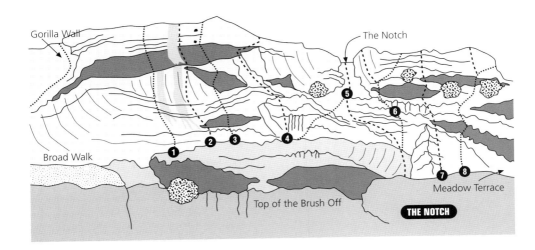

Gorilla Wall

The Notch

Broad Walk

Meadow Terrace

Top of the Brush Off

THE NOTCH

1   Sandy NL 6b *

Climb the overhanging wall just left of the sandy streak from a very difficult start, using tiny pockets to cross the bulge.

2   Evil Uncle Quentin NL 5c

10 feet right of Sandy climb the bulging wall using pockets to cross the top overhang.

3   Shoie McFee NL 5c

8 feet left of Overleaning Wall climb the overhang on friable holds, moving left to finish.

4   Overleaning Wall HVS 5a ⚠

Climb directly above the left hand start of The Notch via a boat-shaped flake. Poor rock.

The next section of the ledge is known as Meadow Terrace and can be reached by an exposed high level traverse.

5   The Notch D *

The obvious sandy notch at the top of the crag can be reached from either ledge. A good top pitch for Little By Little. A direct entry can be made by climbing the sandy roof at the left end of The Meadow at 5b.

6   Tree Wall HVS 5b

Climb the steep wall up to the first of three trees to the right of The Notch, moving right to finish. A more direct finish climbs the small wall to the left at the top at 6a.

7   Arcograph NL 5c

A direct line to the left of the second tree.

8   Arco VS 4c

Climb up over black bulges to the left of the third tree and escape along a rightwards trending ramp. A leftwards finish increases the grade to 5b.

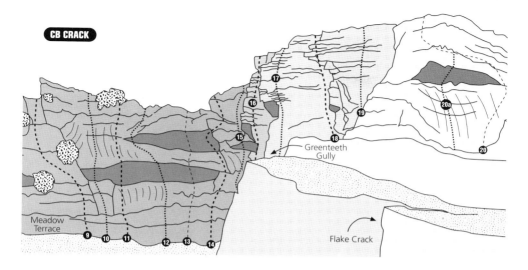

CB CRACK

Greenteeth
Gully

Meadow
Terrace

Flake Crack

9 Terrace Wall D
Climb up the right hand side of the shallow
recess. Alternatively the steep crack on the left
presents more of a challenge.

10 Delilah HVS 5b   ✱
The bulging wall to the right. Start up the small
pillar and climb the pocketed black wall above.

11 Why, Why, Why? NL 6a
Climb the roof to the right at its widest point
and continue directly to the top.

12 Betrayed By A Woman! NL 5c
5 feet to the right is a large hole at ten feet;
climb to this and on directly above.

13 Short Back and Sides NL 5c
Just left of the corner climb past fangs of rock,
over the overhang and trend leftwards to finish
up a slight depression.

14 Samson's Wall E2 5c   ✱ ⚠
The shallow corner best climbed from left to
right via the obvious 'penile' hold. Poor
protection

15 Greenteeth Groove S 4a   ⚠
A grotty crack just left of the upper part of
Greenteeth Gully.

16 Tyro's Wall HVS 5b   ✱✱
Exciting climbing up the black arete left of the
top section of Greenteeth Gully.

17 Black Wall HS 4b   ✱
The short exposed wall left of the flake;
gripping!

18 C.B. Crack VD   ✱
Named due to its resemblance to the flake crack
on Scafell Central Buttress.

19 C.B. Wall VD   ✱
Climb the wall to the right of the crack.

20 The Squirm VD
Start up the ramp to the right of the small roof
then traverse left above this to finish up the
nose. The roof direct is 5c (Route 20a).

21 Spare Moment S   ✱
Pull over the cave at the foot of the small buttress to the right and climb the short wall above.

UPPER WEST BUTTRESS

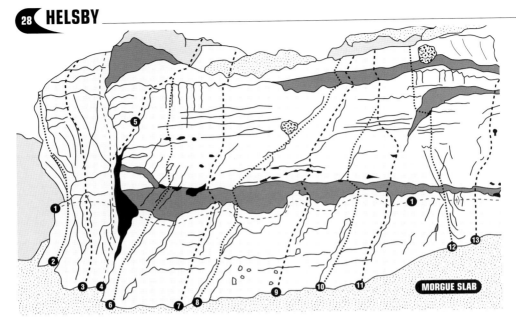

On the lower tier from the foot of Clashooks Gully the crag continues rightwards. This is Lower West Buttress and has some of the best climbing at Helsby.

1   Cloister Traverse S 4a
The obvious break 15ft up is gained from Clashooks Gully and followed to its logical conclusion at the foot of Grooved Slab.

2   Chromium Crack E2 5c
Ascend the overhanging crack above the ledge; a safe lead.

3   Golden Pillar E1 5b   ** ⚠
An excellent committing route up the big pillar. Climb directly up the pillar, moving left to climb with trepidation up the scoop above.

4   The Overhanging Crack VS 4c   *
Climb out of the cave and up the obvious crack.

5   Agag VS 4c   **
Climb out of the cave and up the crack on the wall to the right.

6   Cadaver Eyes NL 6b   *
A hard route up over the roof and blank slab to the right of Agag.

7   Magical Charm NL 6a   *
Another hard line up the big green slab with some long reaches and a hard mantel.

8   Morgue Slab E2 5b   ** ⚠
A great route up the centre of the big slab. Follow the diagonal fault and cross the roof at the weakest point.

9   Necrophiliac NL 6a   *
Climb the roof to the right just above an obvious pillar.

10 Project ?   *
Climb the roof further right just left of a faint leaning crack.

11 Dog on a String NL 6c
The hardest route at Helsby? Climb the black overhanging wall using a broken/chipped hold, trend right to the top. (a.k.a.'Beatdave')

12 The Beatnik E5 6a   ***
A historic route. Must be climbed with a hangover, flared jeans and a headband!

13 240 Volt Shocker NL 6c
Ascend the wall to the right utilising the obvious 'Light Bulb' hold.

LOWER WEST BUTTRESS

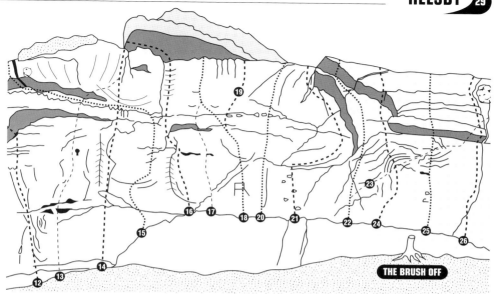

THE BRUSH OFF

There are many short boulder problems on the bottom slab if it ever gets cleaned. The low traverse is worth doing at 5b. Finish at the bottom of the Beatnik.

14 Twin Scoops E1 5c *
Layback precariously up the flakes then climb directly up the scoop above.

15 The Gangway S 4a *
Balance across the slab rightwards, tricky! Climb the scoop then traverse left a long way along the break to finish up a short deep crack.

16 Grooved Slab HS 4b ***
A great climb which almost featured in Classic Rock!

17 The Brush Off Direct E4 6a *
Teeter up the middle of the wall to join The Brush Off higher up.

18 The Brush Off E4 5c ***
A classic slab climb. Use the chipped graffiti to start, then move left to a gripping finale!

19 Alternative Finish E5 6a *
An extremley thin finish up the blank headwall to the right.

20 Jim's Chimney E3 6a **
Nice climbing up 'natural' features to the right. The first bit was the original start to Little By Little before the holds were chipped.

21 Little By Little S 4a
Gain the ledge using the chipped holds, then climb the corner above to a sandy finish.

22 Oyster Slab Super Direct HS 5a *

23 Oyster Slab S 4a
Find the easiest way up and across the obvious slab to finish up right of Trojan Crack. A poor route.

24 Oyster Slab Direct VS 4b
A better route which climbs directly to the undercuts then trends left up the wall above.

25 Route III Oyster Slab VS 5b *
Climb the wall just to the left of Trojan Crack next to the 'Free Stuart Christie' graffiti using the obvious pocket and two small undercuts.

26 Trojan Crack S 4a
The deep corner crack, in a dreadful state.

LOWER WEST BUTTRESS

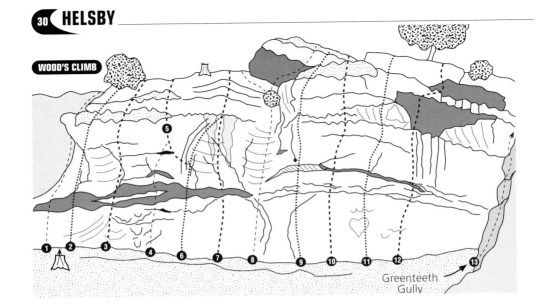

WOOD'S CLIMB

1 Trojan Nose S 4a
Teeter up the blunt nose right of the crack and on to a grassy ledge.

2 Waterloo Wall E2 5c
Gain the tiny ledge on the wall right of the nose; hard work for the grade!

3 Unknown NL 6a
Climb into the scoop and exit right using pockets.

4 Fragile Wall Direct E2 6a
A difficult alternative start to Fragile Wall; over the roof and directly up the wall above.

5 Fragile Wall LH E2 5b
Climb the corner and exit left via the obvious hole to join the previous route.

6 Fragile Wall E3 5c ★★
Climb the corner then continue up the shallow curving groove on fragile edges. A serious lead.

7 Daniel E2 5c ★
The wall to the right taken direct via two small layaways.

8 Wood's Climb HVS 5a ★★★
Classic! Climb the central hanging groove line to exit left or right at the roof.

9 The Unknown Arete NL 6a ★
The blunt arete just to the right via a long reach.

10 Party Blues E4 6b ★ ⚠
Climb the centre of the wall crossing the small overlap at the obvious flake.

11 Unknown NL 6b ★
Climb the wall to the right using the short smooth layaway crack.

12 The Runnel NL 6b ★★
Difficult moves up the shallow runnels and direct over the left edge of the roof above. Sadly now chipped.

This whole section of wall can be traversed along the obvious break at a pumpy 5a! There are also a couple of boulder problems using chipped features underneath Party Blues.

13 Greenteeth Gully Mod 2 ★
A classic of the genre! Climb the central chimney ignoring the sand, small children and dogs coming in the other direction. A more difficult variation takes the exciting rib on the right at the top.

LOWER WEST BUTTRESS

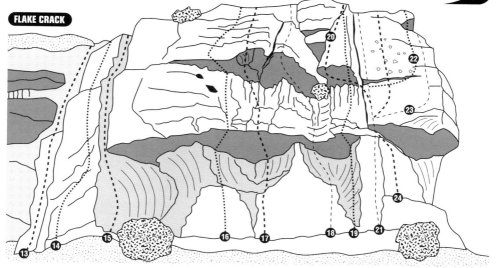

FLAKE CRACK

14 Swings VS 5a ★★
Climb the delicate shimmering green wall using the left edge of the crack. (E2 5c without the crack!)

15 Greenteeth Crack S 4b
Oh dear, it's time you realised this is what traditional climbing is all about! Good training for Yosemite only much shorter!

16 Dinnerplate Crack S 4b ★★
Altogether more pleasant moves up the flake over the roof, then past the remains of the old Dinnerplate flake itself which sticks out of the wall above.

17 Ho Ho Ho E3 6a
Climb the difficult line between the two cracks.

18 Twin Caves Crack S 4b ★★
More good climbing over the roof to the right.

19 Flake Arete NL 6a/b
Climb the right hand side of the roof then directly up the arete.

20 Flake Innominate E2 5c ★
Climb up Flake Crack until you can step left and take the thin buttress directly, utilising a handy diagonal fault.

21 Flake Crack VS 5a ★★★
A sandstone classic. Climb the dusty pillar to the base of a long corner, then hand jam or layback to the top. See photo.

22 Foolish Finish E4 5c ★ ⚠
Climb up Flake Crack to the break, traverse right and finish up the arete.

23 Licentious Jug E5 6a ★ ⚠
Even more foolish. Traverse to the arete at a lower level, then teeter upwards to the top in an exposed position; alternativley climb the wall direct from halfway along the traverse. Another variant is to climb the roof just right of Flake Crack without using the crack at 6b.

24 Flake Wall E5 6a ★★★ ⚠
The final variation is possibly the best and certainly the longest route on this section of the wall. Start under the big roof, climb up the short dusty crack, step left and pull over as for Flake Crack; then step right and climb the centre of the pocketed wall directly. Excellent climbing. It is also possible to start up the curving flake under the roof at the same grade. Graded using gear in Flake Crack.

LOWER WEST BUTTRESS

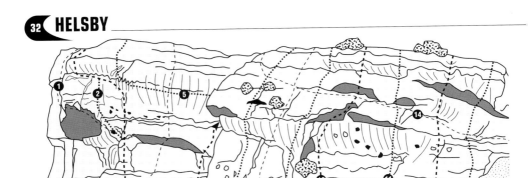

1 Black Hole Arete NL 6b ★★
A hard eliminate which climbs up Calcutta Wall and then traverses along the lip all the way to the arete. An alternative finish can be made up the short crack halfway along the traverse.

2 Calcutta Wall E4 5c ★★ ⚠
A difficult and strenuous route which starts up the pillar then swings left over the roof utilising the 'Black Hole' to regain the traverse of Eliminate 1.

3 Eliminate 1 E1 5b ★★★
An excellent pitch with an exposed and gripping finish which is usually sandy! Climb the pillar to a collection of spikes, then traverse left and up a short slab to the top.

4 Cinemascope NL 6b ★
A hard climb up the wall through The Wendigo to the top.

5 The Wendigo E3 5c ★★ ⚠
This is the name given by North American Indians to a type of evil spirit! Make a difficult traverse out of the chimney to the spikes of Eliminate 1 then finish directly on rounded holds above.

6 Easy Chimney M
The obvious chimney is gained from the right.

7 End Crack VD
Climb up the scoops then continue up the dirty crack above; hard for the grade!

8 The Parasol VS 5a
Straight up the wall left of The Umbrella.

9 The Umbrella E2 5c ★
Climb the strenuous pocketed wall over the bulge just left of the cave.

10 Parapluie E1 5b ★
Climb out of the cave and directly up the wall above, on suspect rock.

11 The Wart E1 5b
Reach the good holds above the right hand side of the cave, then move left to an undercut and climb the wall above.

12 Angel's Face E1 5b
Right of a small cave is a semi-circular groove; climb to this and above.

13 Ape's Crack HVS 5b
Climb the wall and bulge, using a short slanting crack above the start of Ape's Amble.

14 Ape's Amble HS 4b ★
From the right side of the crag gain the obvious leftward traverse. Follow the break with increasing difficulty until a finish can be made up Easy Chimney.

LOWER WEST BUTTRESS

Other Buttresses

20 metres right of the main crag at a similar level is a small buttress with a good 5b problem up the centre. 30 metres beyond this (slightly lower down the hill) is another small buttress with three good problems; these are 5c, 6a and 5a respectively. 200 metres further right, just below the path which runs along the top of the hill, lies a more extensive buttress, the left hand end of which has many good but short problems and traverses. The right hand end

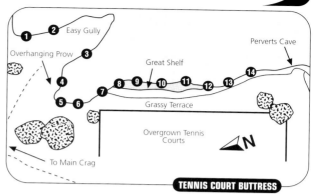

is higher forming a small cave. A 5c climbs the obvious friable flake; the roof to the right can be climbed directly at 6b.

Tennis Court Buttress

This impressive buttress is at a lower level than the main crag and can be found by dropping down to the main path halfway down the hillside and following this for 300 metres until a spectacular prow becomes visible on the left. The buttress lies mainly above a derelict tennis court on private land, legal access remains unclear.

1   Green Buttress VD
The small buttress on the left of the gully.

2   Green Wall VS 4b
The wall to the right of the previous route.

3   Kind Colonel's Crowborough HVS 5b
Start at the foot of the right wall of the gully in a corner. After a few moves swing up and right and finish up the wall.

4   Hangover E1 5c   ✱
The tremendous overhanging prow with a spectacular finish around the nose.

5   Overhang E1 5b
Climb the edge of the overhang.

6   Bad Man's Birchen E1 5b
Five feet right of the tip of the prow. Straight up on rounded holds, moving right at the top.

7   Derek's Disaster HVS 5a
The obvious weakness fifteen feet right of the last route.

8   Fontainbleau HVS 5a
Nothing like its name. Start just right of the previous route and climb the shallow corner, moving left to climb the wall.

9   Niche Wall E1 5b
Start fifteen feet left of the obvious chimney; climb to the ledge up and right, gain the niche on the left and finish above.

10   Alex E1 5b
Start as for the last route and then ascend the slab directly above the ledge.

11   Trespasser Chimney E1 5b
Start below the obvious chimney, climb up to it and then climb up it. Enough said.

12   Deuce E1 5c
To the right of the chimney is a corner and roof crack. Climb the corner with ease and then struggle like hell with the crack and continue up the wall direct.

13   Wimbledon Wall E1 5b
Climb the overhanging wall right of the previous route to finish through a scoop.

14   Grand Slam E2 5c
Climb the roof at its widest point.

The Amphitheatre Traverse travels along the obvious shelves at the back of the Amphitheatre. The Girdle Traverse is from left to right and starts up Green Buttresses and joins Amphitheatre Traverse.

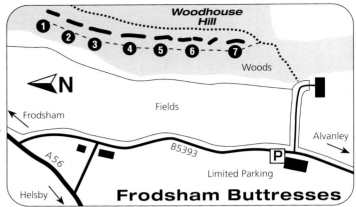

1 St Stepen's Buttress
2 Great Wall
3 Cinema Screen
4 Cave Buttress
5 Long Buttress
6 Changing Room Buttress
7 Hoop-La Buttress

Frodsham Buttresses

GENERAL

Right then, first things first! The crags are not on Frodsham Hill but on Woodhouse Hill which is the highest of the group of three. Secondly, as well as being on the wrong damned hill, many have argued that it is at the wrong angle, but do not believe them! They are not, they are wonderful and along with Pex Hill offer the best bouldering in the area.

ASPECT

The climbing is on a series of isolated buttresses ranging in height from 10-30ft along the upper part of the hill. They make a great summer evening venue as they catch the sun at this time of the day. They can stay damp in the winter months but if a good wind is up they can soon become climbable. One problem is the thick covering of leaves in the summer period which can prevent drying after rain. Frodsham climbing is usually very steep and on good holds; the rock is solid but there are a few fragile bits which an experienced climber will easily spot. A general rule is that when the rock is particularly sandy, take care.

APPROACH

When travelling towards Helsby from Frodsham on the A56, take a left turn just after passing The Netherton Arms on the right. This is Tarvin Road (signposted to Alvanley). Travel on this road for one mile until a converted farmhouse and barn is reached on the right. There is enough room for TWO CARS

ONLY to park discreetly; there have been problems with parking in this area so please be sensible. Additional parking is available 200 yards further along the road on the left and further still at the T junction another 100 yards beyond this. Opposite the farmhouse is a narrow road which leads to the base of the hill; walk along here, through the kissing gate and climb up the hillside. When you reach the top turn left on to a wide and well trodden path; the crags lie below. The buttresses are described from left to right, so continue along the path until you reach the edge of a golf course. The first buttress, St.Stephen's, lies below.

Continuing along the top path past the golf course, down some stone steps and along a lower path brings you to a small quarried area on the right. A few problems and short routes have been climbed here; the right arete is a good 5b and climbing into the small cave - 'Tom Thumb's Hole' - to have one's photogragh taken is a must.

Further on and up 'Jacob's Ladder' or the 'Baker's Dozen Steps' the path continues towards Beacon Hill and the Mersey View. After about 300 yards the discerning crack climber will be rewarded by finding Banner's 'Helter Skelter Crack' (5c) at the back of a wooded cove. There are numerous small and broken buttresses further on which are of little interest.

Right: Dave Johnson cruising up Crew's Arete 5b,
Cave Buttress Frodsham.
photo: Alan Cameron-Duff

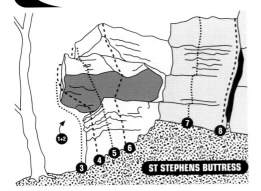

The first buttress of any signifigance is just below the path about 200 yards along the hill-top. There are other buttresses visible above the path in the trees, none of them are worthy of investigation, being composed of softer and more friable rock.

1   St. Stephen's Wall 4b
Climb the wall to the left of the roof.

2   Left Wall 5c
The wall just left of the arete.

3   Mexican Bob 6a
A hard eliminate which climbs the left arete.

4   The Long Lurch 5a   ******
Climb directly through the centre of the roof, a classic problem.

5   Rick's Reach 5c
Climb the nose of the buttress.

6   Right Hand Route 5a
Climb the rounded arete/roof to the right.

7   Big Wall 4c
Climb the pleasant wall to the right.

8   Deep Crack 4b
Climb it if you dare. A good problem climbs the right wall of Deep Crack without using this or the crack on the right at 5c.

9   Twin Cracks D
The obvious crack a few feet further on.

A little further on the ground drops away beneath a large steep wall. This is Great Wall, the largest and most intimidating of the buttresses at Frodsham.

1   Left Arete 5b
Trundle up near the left arete.

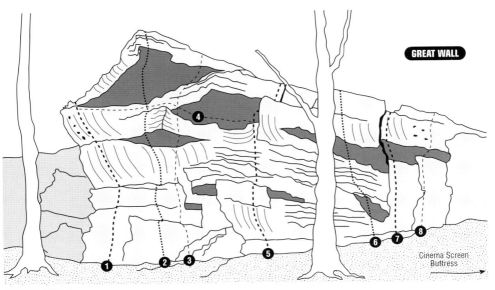

GREAT WALL

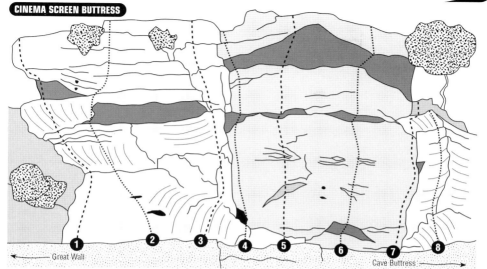

CINEMA SCREEN BUTTRESS

2   Tom's Roof NL 6b
Straight up the wall and over the big roof.

3   Unknown 5c   *
Climb up the wall to the big roof and escape out right.

4   Left Hand Route 5c
Start up Great Wall then traverse left under the big roof to safety.

5   Great Wall 5c   ***
Climb up the centre of the wall into the corner, then traverse out right to gain the wall above.

6   Iron Dish Wall 5c   ***
Good committing climbing up the wall right of the tree.

7   Frodsham Crack 5a
Fist jam or make a long reach to ascend the obvious crack

8   Unknown Wall 6a
A difficult and scary problem takes the wall right of the crack.

Before reaching the next buttress there are several pleasant problems on the mossy slabs. The next buttress bears a faint resemblance to a cinema screen; unfortunately the rock on the 'screen' is of poor quality.

1   Slanting Crack D

2   Slab Route 5a
Climb the first slab then step left to avoid the roof to gain the second.

3   Cinema Arete 4c   *

4   Birch Tree Corner 4a

5   Multi-Screen 6a   * ⚠
A difficult direct on fragile holds.

6   Central Route 5c   *
Another fragile route.

7   Cracked Corner 4b   *

8   Arete Route 5b   *
Technical moves up the nice arete.

The low traverse from Birch Tree Corner to finish up Arete Route is 6a, the upper one is 5c. The next rock to be encountered is Cave Buttress.

CAVE/CINEMA SCREEN BUTRESS

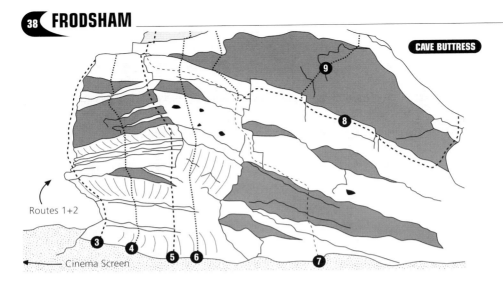

CAVE BUTTRESS

Routes 1+2

Cinema Screen

1   Corner And Traverse VD   *
Climb the short corner then traverse right to the arete.

2   Left Wall 5a   *
The fine wall on sharp holds.

3   Crew's Arete LH   5c   *
Climb directly up the arete.

4   Crew's Arete 5b   ***
Follow in the great man's footsteps. A superb little route up the wall and left over the square cut roof.

5   Superdirect 5a   *
Climb the arete directly.

6   Superwall 5b   *
Ascend the wall to the right on pockets; after a problematic start.

7   Ordinary Route VD
It is also possible to finish more directly at VS.

8   Leo's Traverse 5a
Climb out of the cave then traverse rightwards under the roof. Nasty landing.

9   I Was a Teenage Caveman 6c NL   *
Climb directly out of the centre of the cave and climb across the big roof on creaking flakes.

CAVE BUTTRESS

A few yards from Cave Buttress is Mangrove Slab S, when clean perhaps the best of the few slab climbs at Frodsham. Beyond this a small steep buttress of rock comes into view; this is The Prow.

1   The Scoop S
Climb the short corner and scoop.

2   Twin Cracks 5a/b
Climb the undercut crack in the centre of the wall to a ledge, then the thin crack above.

3   The Prow 5b   **
An excellent route which climbs the steepest section of the wall from the left to a fine finish.

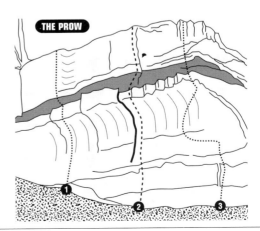

THE PROW

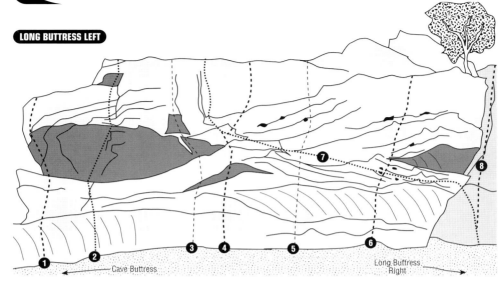

LONG BUTTRESS LEFT

Cave Buttress

Long Buttress Right

After crossing a grassy gully just before Long Buttress, a small green wall provides scope for two small routes - one up the centre (4a), the other just right of the left hand arete (4a). Slightly further along the path is Long Buttress which is quite extensive and has some short but worthwhile routes, occasionally with poor landings.

1   Arete Route 5b
The overhang and hanging arete.

2   Jimmy's Crack 5c   ★★★
An excellent route. Bold moves lead out over the roof on creaking flakes.

3   Direct Route 5b   ★
Nice climbing on big holds up the steep wall to the right.

4   Heather Wall Direct 5a
Climb over the roof at its right end to join the top of Heather Wall.

5   Donkey Route Direct 5b

6   Heather Variant 4c
Up the wall just left of the shelf.

7   Heather Wall 4a
Climb up to the shelf on the left of the chimney; traverse left then finish up an awkward wall.

8   Chimney Route S
The obvious feature provides the kind of struggle one would expect.

9   Tank Top 6a   ★
The arete of Sweater direct on the left, scary.

10 Sweater 5b   ★
Climb the roof then the right hand side of the arete above on pockets.

11 Pullover 5b   ★★★
The classic of the crag, a committing pull over the roof followed by some delicate moves left on the wall above.

12 Jumper 5c   ★
An eliminate between Pullover and Thin Crack.

LONG BUTTRESS

13 Thin Crack Superdirect 5c
A difficult contrived problem climbing the crack directly, eliminating the ledge.

14 Thin Crack 4b ★
Gain the ledge and climb the thin crack above.

15 Left Hand Crack VD

16 Right Hand Crack VD ★
Self-explanatory really!

17 Flake Route VD ★
Pull directly over the small roof 6ft left of the corner, then climb the crack to a difficult mantelshelf finish. A harder variation is to climb the wall on the left all the way (4a).

18 Tree Wall D
Climb the short corner.

A difficult and bizarre boulder problem can be contrived by climbing the ceiling (eliminating the holds on the lip) from beneath the ledge of Thin Crack to finish up Tank Top. An esoteric and pointless 6b+!

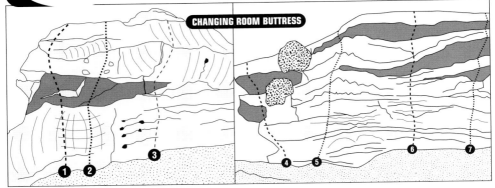

Changing Room Buttress

The next rock of any merit is Changing Room Buttress, split by a vegetated slope.

1 Green Arete 5b *
A miniature classic requiring a bold approach!

2 Central Route 5c *
Diminutive but still scary.

3 The Mantelshelf 5a *
An amusing mantelshelf problem.
The next routes are further on across the vegetated gully.

4 Double Overhang 5a
Immediately right of the gully.

5 Left Hand Route 5a *
From the left of the buttress climb straight up on large holds.

6 Direct Route 5c *
Climb the centre of the wall to a very difficult mantelshelf finish.

7 The Right Hand Route 4a *
Climb out right and up the obvious arete.

There are three main traverses across the buttress which are usually chalked up. The higher traverse is 5a, the middle one is 5c and the lower one which continues around the corner until the buttress runs into the ground is 6b. Further right again another slight buttress provides a short problem up the obvious corner and some interesting bouldering. Further right is Neb Buttress.

Neb Buttress

1 Wall and Traverse D *
The left side of the buttress.

2 Intermediate Route 4b *
Climb the overhang just to the right of the flake.

3 Direct Route 5a *
Climb straight through the roof at its widest point.

4 Neb Route 5c/c *
Start at the foot of the chimney, then either climb leftward across the overhang or directly (5c) over the roof.

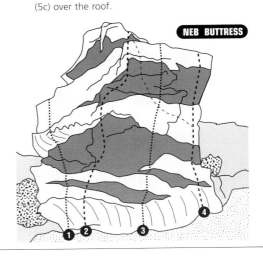

NEB BUTTRESS

NEB BUTTRESS

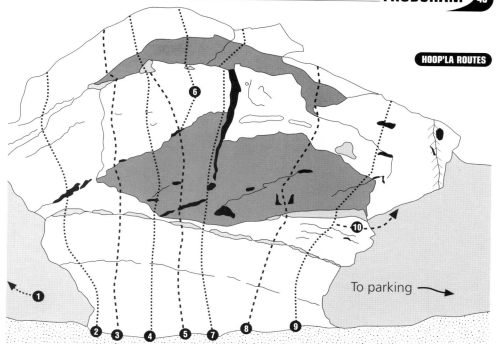

To parking →

Further on the last buttress encountered is Hoop-La identified by a large overhang split by a prominent crack. This offers the best bouldering at Frodsham along with some classic micro-routes.

1 Pants 5a +   *
Climb the roof on the buttress just left of Hoop-La Buttress.

2 The Overhanging Wall 4c   *
The pleasant juggy wall right of the corner.

3 Colton's Crack 6b   *
Climb the roof and thin crack using a finger hold to the right. Don't get your knee stuck!

4 Dave's Route 6c   *

5 Mike's Route 6c   *

6 Pearce's Route 6a   *
From the pockets at the start of Hoop-La Crack move leftward to a pocket on the lip. The secret is a worrying toe jam.

7 The Hoop-La 5b   **
A nice problem taking the obvious weakness through the centre of the roof.

8 Boysen's Route 6a   *
Start right of Hoop-La and work your way out right then back left slightly at the large flake.

9 Banner's Route 5c   **
The right side of the roof to the obvious flake.

10 Tradesman's Entrance 6a
From the jugs on Banner's Route slap right around the arete to a sloping finish.

11 The Overhanging Crack M
The small crack on the right hand side of the buttress (not shown).

12 The Right Wall 5a
Climb the wall to the right of the crack on good holds (not shown).

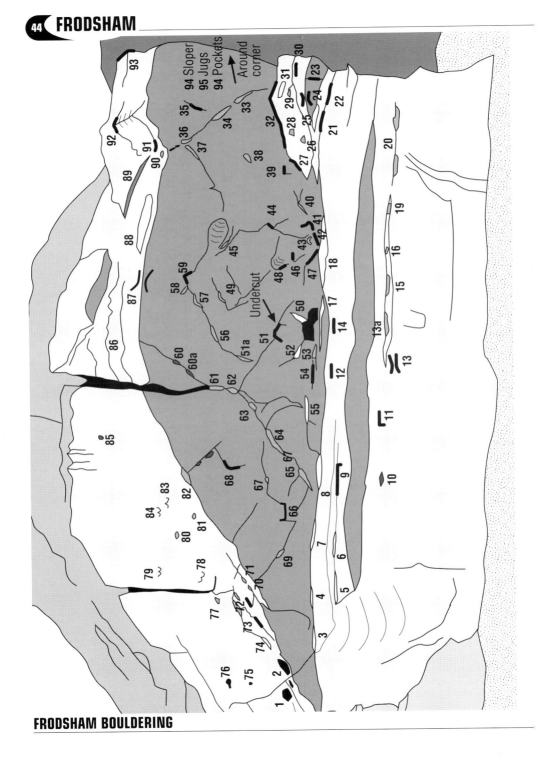

94 Sloper
95 Jugs
94 Pockets
Around corner

Undercut

The bouldering at Hoopla requires power, technique and a fair amount of either bottle, or good spotting, so take some friends and a big mat. Success is sometimes achieved by using cunning methods such as a foot jam or toe hook, the consequence of this is that you can end up on your back. You have been warned!

1 The Pockets 5c V1
(6) 5, 3, 2, 75, 76, break.

2 Colton's Crack 6a+ V4
(6) 4, 69, 72, 79, break.

3 Johnson's Route 6c V7
(4,7) 70, 81, 80, 84, 83, break.

4 Mike's 6c V7
(64) 67, 82, 84/83, break.

5 The Collin's Crucifix 7a V9+
(51) 56, 87 share, shelf out right.

6 Challenge Chadwick 6b V5
(5) 6, 8, 67, 63, 57, 58, 87, 86, top.

7 Tim The Tiny Timelord 6c V8
(13a) 52, 48, 51a, 56, 60, 86, top.

8 Tim's Teletubby Scooter 6c+ V8+
(13a) 52, 48, 49, 45, 87, (crossover) 86, top.

9 The Ant Hill Mob 6c+ V9
(15) 52 share, 56, 87 share, shelf out right.

10 Musky 6c V7
(15) 50, 48, 59, 86.

11 Catch The Pigeon 6c V7
(18) 44, 48, 59 share, 86, shelf above.

12 Penelope Pitstop 6b V6
(15) 47, 42 (undercuts) 59, 58, 86

13 The Slope 7a V9
(44,39) 88 share, shelf out right.

14 Foghorn Leghorn 6c V8
(18) 44, 36, 37, slap around nose rightwards to 93, top.

15 Deputy Dog 6b V6
(20) 28, 34, 33, 94, 95, top.

16 Tradesman's Entrance 6a V3
(32) 94, 95, top. The same holds footless gets you 6b V5.

17 The Pinch 6b+ V7
(20) 24 pinch, 31(poor sloper) 94,top.

18 Banner's Varient 6a V3
(20) 22, 28, 34, 37, 36, 92, top.

19 The Leap 6a V3
(20) 32.

20 Teletubby In The Oven 6c+ V8+
(25) 24, 38, 35, 90, 93, top.

Traverses

21 The Break 5b V0
The obvious break at chest height.

22 The Lower Break 6a V3
Holds below the break, right to left until 21 can be reached then 22, finish in the crack beyond.

23 Joe's Traverse 6c V8
(1), any hold above or on the lip to 86 then, 92, 93, top.

24 The Indirect 6c V9
(3), 69, 67, 62, 56, 36, 37, 34, 33, 94, 95, top. Or from 36, 37, 93, 95, top, gets V10.

25 The Crossthrough 6a V4
(32), 27, 46, 51, 64, 66, 72.

26 The Ripper 6b V5
(72), 66 share, 64, 62, 61, 56, 59, 36, 37, 91, 92, top.

New Problems

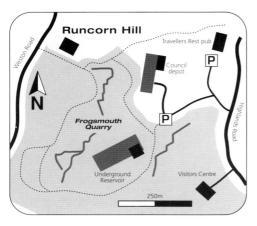

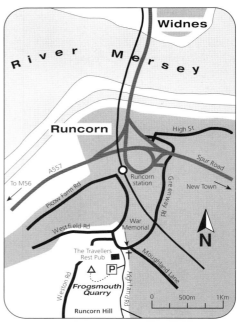

GENERAL

How should I put this? It used to be crap and now it's great, why? The bolt. There were a few good top rope problems worth the trouble and a couple of frightening aid climbs but Frogsmouth was largely ignored for years. It has all changed now and offers a number of very fine bolted climbs on mostly steep walls from 30-60ft high offering technical and reachy climbing.

ACCESS

Runcorn Hill is owned by Halton Borough Council and managed by Mersey Valley Partnership as a park and nature reserve. Local climbers have reached an agreement that to ensure future climbing access in the quarry **climbing should only take place on the walls already developed. Do not climb or abseil over the top.**

ASPECT

The rangers have turned this once filthy quarry into an attractive area used by a number of local people for recreation. Please try not to bawl and scream when your redpoint attempt fails as some of the park's other users have been known to take offence. So take failure as a good little sports climber should; cry, sulk, adopt a new training regime and become a little more sad and socially dysfunctional than you were before.

Check this quarry out in winter as some routes can remain dry after heavy rain. Unfortunately the sandstone is a little soft and brittle, so please take care. Remember also that all the routes will require a thorough cleaning in the spring and after poor weather. Be careful with some of the in situ protection; some of it is rather uninspiring!

APPROACH

The quarry is situated on Runcorn Hill in the town of Runcorn. When approaching from Liverpool, cross the Runcorn Bridge (A533) and turn left heading for Old Runcorn. Do not enter it but take a right into Greenway Road; follow this until a war memorial is reached after approximately two miles. Take the first left after this into Highlands Road. After 70 yards turn into the signposted car park for Runcorn Hill. From the car park walk rightwards down a path until the quarry is seen on the left.

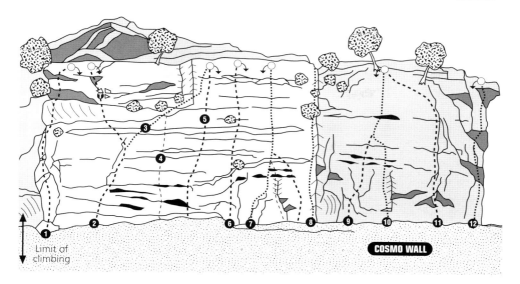

COSMO WALL

Climbing is banned on the first two walls on the far left hand end of the quarry. The next face is Cosmo Wall, characterised by black rock with many horizontal faults.

1 **Dogsbody Arete F6a** ★★
An enjoyable route with a good little roof.

2 **Wall Street F6a+** ★
Take a thread for the top wall.

3 **Fashion Spot F6b**
Camera, lights, action.

4 **Agony Aunt F7a**
One nasty little move!

5 **Zest F6a** ★
Follow the bolts via a chipped hold; take some gear for the first bit. Chipped for giants!

6 **Horoscope F6a**
Similar to the previous route.

7 **Smart Girl Sex Survey F6c+** ★
A good route with three possible starts - up the obvious groove, its right arete or the wall to the left of the groove.

8 **Perfumed Groove HVS 5b**
The obvious dihedral.

9 **Chaturanga Danasana F6b**
A rather dusty climb.

10 **Just After Fifty F6a**
An easier start to the previous route.

11 **Savasana E2 5c**
A pleasant climb on good holds.

12 **Apple Crumble F6a**
Something is crumbling on this climb and it's not apple.

The next face - Viz Wall - is the highest and most impressive in the quarry and has some of the best climbing in the area.

13 **Johnny Fartpants F6c+** ★
Climb past the unusual protection to a hard crux next to the ice screw!

14 **The Flying School F6c+** ★★★
One of the best routes here. Start with a nice mantelshelf and move leftwards for the crux.

COSMO WALL

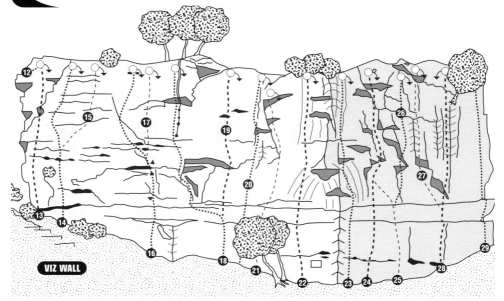

15 Pathetic Sharks F7a ✱
A difficult and scary climb; spot the break with the holds on!

16 Topless Skateboarding Nun F7a+ ✱✱✱
A tremendous route, one of the best in the area. A difficult crack leads to easier ground before the magnificent headwall.

17 The Big Stiff One F7c ✱✱✱
A more direct version of the previous route; one very difficult move bars the way.

18 Comet Crack E5 6a ✱✱
A great crack climb with natural gear protection.

19 Ivan Jellical F6c+ ✱✱
Almost as good as Skateboarding Nun. Both delicate and powerful with a crux move which is easily messed up. Starts direct up the friable wall past a drilled pocket which is hard to spot.

20 Fat Slags F7a+ ✱
A very powerful crux low down leads to long reaches between positive holds.

21 Nude Motorcycle Girl F6c+ ✱
A good climb following the groove.

22 Biffa Bacon F7b
Often dirty. Hard climbing over the concrete encrusted bulges leads to a reachy last move - the crux.

23 Victor Pratt F7a
A dirty but spectacular climb up the imposing corner.

Right of the corner the wall is more broken and dirty.

24 Wear 'em out Wilf F7a
Impressive route up the large wall just right of the corner.

25 Bash Street Kids F7a
Joins the previous route at half height.

26 Dennis the Menace F6c
Start as for 25 but break out rightwards at half height.

27 Keyhole Kate F7a
Follow the line of bolts via the hanging arete.

VIZ WALL

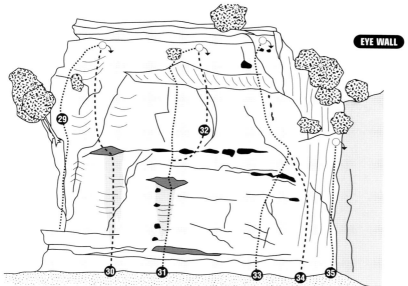

EYE WALL

28 Broken Skull Groove F6c
The obvious groove past a tree.

29 Anaesthetic F6a
Climb the arete using a bucket, spade and ice cream cone.

Around the arete Eye Wall isn't quite as imposing but has some good climbing spoilt only by a sandy break at half height.

30 Street of Shame F7a ★★
A fine climb which unfortunately sports a sandy break.

31 Dear Bill F7a+ ★
A climb which is very difficult if you're short.

32 Ugandan Relations F7a
The same start as the previous route; it breaks out right and climbs the shallow corner.

33 East African Affairs F7a+ ★★
The best route on this wall, with the crux by the second bolt.

34 Murkeyside F6c
A poor alternative start to the previous route.

35 Owl F6c
Thin bridging.

A1 Wall
Forty yards to the right of the last route a small slabby buttress is home to two poor routes.

36 A1 E1 5c
Poor and short.

37 Prodigal Sway E2 5c
Also poor and short.

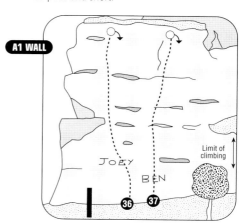

A1 WALL

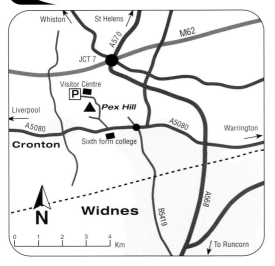

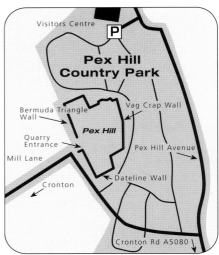

"I read every mag, every book. I missed a few of my O levels. On the day of the Art O level exam I went to Pex Hill". Joe Healey in The Power of Climbing, David Jones.

GENERAL

Suffering from donkey footwork and zero technique? Well invest in a little time at Pex. It has been home to some of the most attractive climbers around (I am talking technique here). The routes require clean and precise movement if success is to be achieved; climb like a mule and you will land on your butt.

ACCESS

When toproping **Do not use the railings** as the water board will slap your wrist. After bouldering use a soft tooth brush to clean the holds; please do not use wire brushes as sandstone is very easily damaged. Abseilers should wear training shoes or similar footwear rather than big boots. In the past the quarry has suffered a litter problem, so please take all your rubbish with you.

Quarrying began in the 16th century and reached a peak in the 19th, with work finally ceasing in 1893. During the Second World War the quarry was used for target practice, which is how some of those wonderful rounded pockets were formed (some still contain bullets). Every 20 years the reservoir at the top of the hill is drained into the quarry. Don't be caught on Pipe Down when the floodgates open!

PEX HILL INTRODUCTION

For a hole in the dirt Pex is rather attractive due to a good ranger service that maintains the park. Let's try and keep it that way. I can remember times when the quarry acted as an unofficial needle exchange and dumping ground for stolen cars! Pex Hill Environmental Education Centre is managed by Knowsley Parks and Countryside Service and North West Water. For further information contact 0151 495 1410. An observatory is also located at Pex Hill managed by Liverpool Astronomical Society; visits can be arranged through the rangers on the above number.

ASPECT

Walls face all directions and thus sun or shade can be followed all day long. Pex Hill is well known for its ability to dry very quickly after rain although Pex Wall and Main Wall are prone to seepage in the winter. The walls vary in height from 15-45ft, most of the climbs are either sooled or top-roped. Notable climbs worth leading are mentioned in the text.

APPROACH

Pex Hill lies off the A5080 which runs between junction 6 of the M62 and the district of Farnworth in Widnes. On this road, just before entering the village of Cronton when travelling west, is the Widnes Sixth Form College. Opposite this are the old gate posts which are the entrance to Pex Hill. Go to the parking area at the top of the hill and then walk down on the central path until you see the quarry railings. There is only one entrance to the quarry, this is at its lowest point.

outdoor pursuits Widnes

climbing & camping equipment

We sell

Wild Country, Terra Nova, Rab, Edelweiss, HB, Petzl, Camp, Troll, Mountain Equipment, DMM Ordnance Survey, guidebooks, North Cape, Optimus, Coleman, camping gas, Gelert, Ron Hill and much more . . .

Open Tuesday to Saturday 10am-5pm
42 Widnes Road, Widnes, WA8 6AP
Tel: 0151 424 2225

Discounts for local clubs, BMC
and large orders, the best range of technical
rock and ice gear in the area

Call or write for a price list

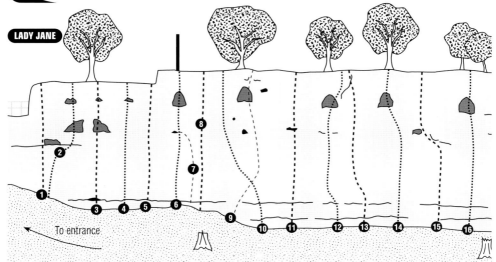

LADY JANE

To entrance

Lady Jane Wall is the long green wall on the left as you walk into the quarry. Even though the wall is often a luminous green due to the canopy of trees, it provides some of the best and the hardest routes at Pex.

1   Too Bold for Steve Boot 5b

2   Set Square 4c
The direct start 'Get Set' is 5c.

3   Tequila Sunrise 5c   *

4   Harvey Warbanger 5b   *

5   Black Russian 6a
The wall to the right taken direct. Reachy.

6   Lew's Leap 5b   **
Did he leap or was he pushed?

7   Lew's Leap Direct 5c
Harder and more indirect version of the original without the big pocket.

8   Finger-Ripper 6b

9   Bermuda Triangle 6a   **
A lot better than the song. The starting holds have got bigger over the years.

This section has a number of traverses. The highest starts up Steve Boot and follows the pockets right to finish up Lew's Leap, 5b. The mid height traverse is also 5b. The low traverse starts at Tequila Sunrise and finishes up Bermuda Triangle 6a. A continuation to the foot of Monobloc is 6c.

10 Cosine Alternative 6a+

11 Breakaway 6c   *
The cutting edge of crimping!

12 Catalepsy 6b   ***
Classic.

13 Monoblock 7a   ***
The hardest route at Pex, with holds so small they can't be seen unless they have chalk on!

14 Bernie 6b   **
Not quite as hard; one of Pex Hill's only sport climbs! Only Joking.

15 Termination 6c
A desperate move left to a large pocket provides the crux.

16 Philharmonic 6b
The tall can reach past the difficulties.

LADY JANE WALL

TWIN SCOOPS

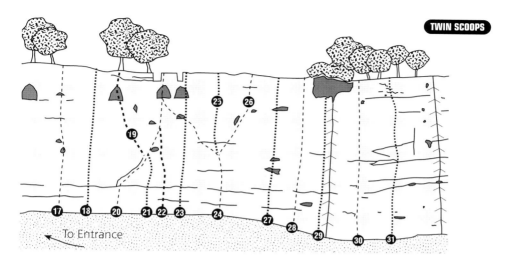

To Entrance →

17 Algripper 5c ★★
Excellent moves between crimps. The crux is low down, rocking over to gain the second pocket. Don't fall onto the tree stump!

18 Jurassic Pork 6b
Direct up the wall, thin.

19 Crossbow 5c
Climb the ramp and move left and finish through the scoop.

20 Lady Jane 5c ★★
A great little climb, up the ramp and good pockets to the top.

21 Lady Jane Direct 5c ★
Without the ramp.

22 Sidestep 5c ★
The wall to the hole via two small edges.

23 Twin Scoops Direct 6a ★
A tricky mantel and big stretch gains the right hand scoop directly.

24 Twin Scoops 4c ★★
A very popular way up and down this section of the cliff!
An enjoyable traverse can be made from the foot of Monoblock to the start of Unicorn at 5a.

25 Twin Scoops RH 5b
The ledges and wall above.

26 Creeping Jesus 5b ★★
Mantel up the ledges, gain the finger slot to the right, then commit yourself to the wall above. A more direct version avoiding the ledges on the left can be climbed at 5c.

27 Kitt's Wall 6b ★★
The big wall to the right via some technical moves.

**28 The Black Pimp
From Marseilles 6b** ★
Named after an interesting character the first ascentionist met on a train! Easier for giants.

29 Unicorn 5b ★★
A good route up the faint arete. Exit left out of the cave avoiding the brambles.

30 Cave Route Right Hand 6b
Eliminate in nature, climb up to the obvious square pocket just right of the cave.

31 Ladytron 5c ★★
This one doesn't get soloed often!

TWIN SCOOPS

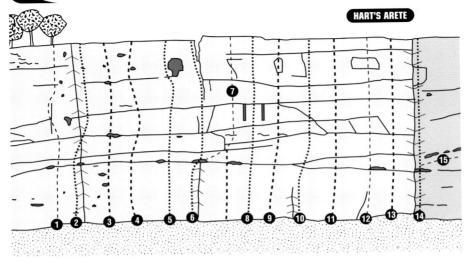

HART'S ARETE

1 Cardiac Arete 6b ★★
Difficult moves to the first break lead to a
boulder problem crux after the large jug.

2 Hart's Arete 6a ★★
Brilliant climbing up the big intimidating arete.
The moves up to the break form a good boulder
problem 6a; for just using the sidepulls award
yourself 6b! Can be led at E4.

3 Zigger Zagger 5b ★★ ⚠
Long reaches between breaks to an interesting top out.

There are three traverses on this section. The
highest travels the obvious break/ledge from
Unicorn to Peeler, 5c+. The middle one is the
classic Hart's Arete Traverse; with feet a few feet
from the ground traverse from Unicorn to Crack
and Up, 6a. The Grand Horizontal is a very low
trraverse underneath the previous one, it starts
at Unicorn and finishes at Hart's Arete, 6c. a low
continuation to The Web is also 6c.

4 Big Greenie 5c ★
The wall just right of Zigger Zagger.

5 The Hulk 5c
Climb direct to the scoop just below the top.

6 Crack and Up 5b ★★
A fine climb. Gain and climb the crack.

7 Corner and Overhang 5b
Start as for Crack and Up; move right at the first
break and ascend the wall above.

8 McArthur Park 5b ★
There is also a boulder problem to the left of the
start using the twin depressions (6a)

9 Eliminate One 5b

10 The Abort 5a ★
Good climbing with the crux at the top.

11 Eliminate Two 5c

12 One Step 5a ★

13 Eliminate Three 5c
The wall just left of the corner.

14 The Web 5b ★★
Nice moves up the big corner, usually damp.
The entire wall can be traversed along the
obvious horizontal break. Can be led at HVS.

15 Pex Wall 6a
The longest route at Pex. Climb up The Web and
follow the rising break rightward to finish up the
final few feet of Warlord.

HART'S ARETE-THE WEB

THE WEB/PEX WALL

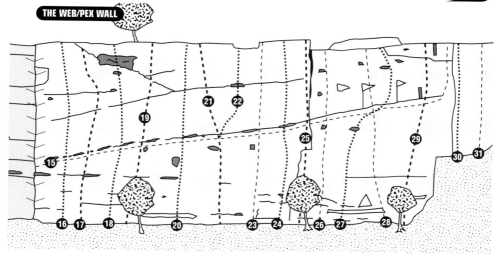

16 Eliminate Four 5c
The wall just right of the corner.
The next couple of routes have benefited greatly from a good cleaning. Climb them and keep them that way.

17 The Witch 5b ★★

18 Four Jays 5b

19 The Wizard 5b ★★

20 Green Monster 6a
A thin top headwall.

21 Alchemy 6a
A hard start through an obvious hole leads to a good finish on small sharp pockets.

22 Warlock 5c ★
Trend right at the top.

23 Warcry 6b
The thin wall just to the right.

24 Warmonger 6b
A few feet right again; similar to the last route.

25 Cobweb Crack 5c ★
Good, but always damp. Can be led at E3.

The next three routes share excellent rock above the top break and deserve more traffic.

26 Spiderman 6b ★
The wall just right of Cobweb. Do not touch that route.

27 Warlord 6a ★
Traverse right slightly at the break to finish

28 The Pacifist 6b+
Difficult right to left line.

29 Innocent 6a+
The wall just left of Peeler.

30 Peeler 5b
The damp crack.

The next four routes need a thorough cleaning to be climbable; is it worth it?

31 Vibrator 5b
The small wall to the right.
Batteries not included.

32 Trident 5a
Just left of the corner. Somewhere.

33 Right Corner 3a
The scrappy corner. The worst route at Pex?

1 Philanderer 4b
Almost as bad, the thin wet crack 20ft right.

2 Massey Street 5b
The crack to the right; up and into the vegetation.

3 Wod's Slot 5c
Climb to the obvious slot in the wall.

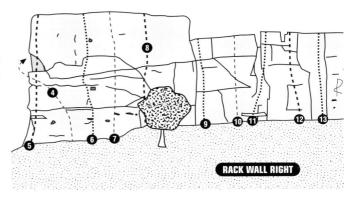

RACK WALL RIGHT

4 Key of the Door 4b
Start around the corner and traverse into the cave and then exit left following the traverse line to the top of the crag. Dirty but very good.

5 Gaming Club 5a ⭐⚠
Climb the spectacular but disposable arete.

Traverses: A good traverse at a height of 5 feet travels from 1 to 4 at 5c.

6 Sandinista 5c
Directly up to the first niche and straight above.

7 Fallout Zone 6a
Hard moves over the second overhang.

8 Pure Mania 6a
Up the obvious black wall.

9 Casino Club 5a
A good little climb, not much of a gamble.

10 The Talisman 4c
Direct up the wall.

A number of traverses start from the arete of Gaming Club and usually finish at The Rack. There are many variations along the way (some of these are described) but the most obvious line along the break is 5b at its most difficult.

11 A Route 3a
What a route, what a name. The obvious chimney.

12 B Route 3a
The groove to the right.

13 Bramble 5a
Dirty corner groove just to the right.

Traverses: the short wall can be crossed at three different heights; the obvious ledge at 4c, the pockets just below at 6a and the lowest with feet a foot from the ground at 6b.

14 Ramble 4c
Up the wall on pockets to the flake crack near the top.

15 Short Crack 4b
Up to and beyond the crack.

PHILANDER WALL

PHILANDER WALL

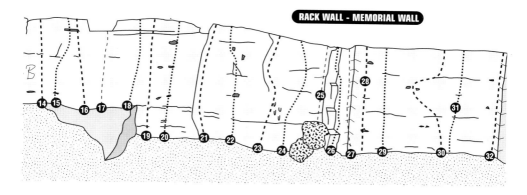

RACK WALL - MEMORIAL WALL

16 Heather Wall 5b
Climb the wall trending slightly leftwards.

17 Bon Ami 5a
Direct up the wall to the right.

18 Bon Gre Malgre 5b
A nice wall climb with a poor landing should you
fall. Start from the edge of the ledge.

19 Master Race 6a+
A hard route with a gripping crux mantel.

20 The Rack 5a ***
A real gem although it is now getting polished.
A difficult eliminate has been climbed between
The Rack and Pipedown -The Wall- at 6b.
There are two good traverse of The Rack wall;
the lowest steps off the ledge on the left and is
5b. The higher one climbs out of Bon Gre Mal-
gre and follows the obvious break at a scary 5b.

21 Pipedown 5c
The often wet crack.

22 Thumbscrew 5b *
Climb the wall five feet to the right of the
previous route.

23 Iron Maiden 5c **
Up to and through the crescent scoop. Needs
cleaning!

24 Garotte 5b
The wall to the right, trending right to finish.

25 Bon Bon 4a
The damp corner. Uninspiring.

26 Gazebo 5a
Wall right of the corner

Memorial Wall

27 Sweeney Arete 5a **
A very good climb.

28 Robbery 5b *
The wall to the right without using the arete.

29 Headstone 6a
The wall two feet to the right. You will need a
good head.

30 Memorial Wall 4b *
From a ledge trend leftwards to a sharp pocket
and then finish rightwards via a ledge.

31 Tombstone 5a
The wall just right.

32 Memorial Corner 4b
The short damp corner.

Vag Crap Wall
The long wall to the right becomes less inspiring
further from the corner. Watch out for dirty top
outs!

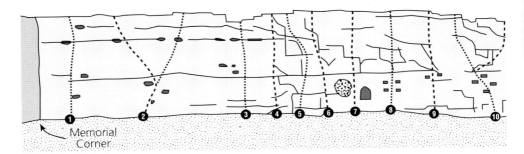

Memorial Corner

1 Hunter's Walk 5b *
Climb the wall on pockets four feet right of the corner.

2 St Paul 5c+
Start below an obvious large pocket and from here finish either right or left.

3 Weasel 5b
One for the rodents.

4 Ferret 5a
More of the same.
Traverses: Vag Crap Traverse, a classic at 6a from Memorial Corner to Ferret; the low level version is 6c with feet a foot from the dirt.

5 Swinging Gulch 4b
A better route with nice moves up the finishing flake.

6 Stoolie 4c

7 Judder 4c

8 Four Most 4c
Climb past the four obvious holds.

9 OK Blue Eyes 4c *
Climb direct past the two shot holes; better than most on this section of the wall.

10 Sabre Cut 4c
Named after the crack up which it is finished. It is also possible to finish out right.

11 Pink Panther 5a
Into the scoop and beyond.

12 Hookey 5b
Easier than it looks; links the two scoops in the pinky looking wall.

13 Pink Wall 6a
A good but neglected route.

14 Pink Corner 4c *
One for the boys!

15 Bill 5a
Poor wall climb seven feet to the right of the corner.

16 Ben 5c
More of the same.

17 The Belcher 6a
Difficult and short wall five feet to the right. To the right the climbs become much easier and these have been left for the visitor to discover.

Right: A young Phil Davidson climbing his own route Catalepsy in 1981.
photo: Ken Travis

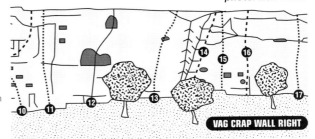

VAG CRAP WALL

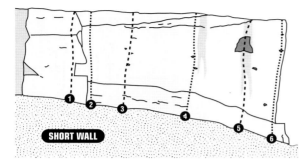

SHORT WALL

1   Blob 3c
Direct up the arete.

2   Cob 4a
The corner.

3   Short Wall 4b
Climb the wall 6 feet right of the corner.

4   Hot Aches 5c
Climb the centre of the wall. The first ascent was a cold one.

5   Marble Eye 5a
Climb direct to the obvious scoop.

The next area has some of the largest and most impressive walls in the quarry and some of the best routes in the area.

6   The Knife 6a   ★★★
A classic arete climb with the crux at the top.

7   Catemytes Crack 6b   ★★
Up the centre of the wall via a shallow corner, passing two dirty pockets at the top.
Originally led with 2 pegs at E5

8   Main Wall 6b   ★★
Start as for Catemytes and then traverse rightwards past an old peg at half height to finish up Staminade.

9   Staminade 6b   ★★★
When clean this is a contender for the best route in the area.

Climb the initial wall on pockets to a hard move to gain the faint arete; finish up this.

10   Lemonade 6b
Climb the dirty wall ten feet to the right of Staminade.

11   Pernod and Black 6b
Another dirty route which would be a good climb with more traffic.

12   Rum and Cocaine 6b
Climb the wall five feet to the left of the corner.

13   One of These Days Direct 5c   ★
Difficult bridging leads to better holds on the mother route.

14   One of These Days 5c   ★★
Start at a letter box hold midway between the corner and Dateline Crack; climb the wall above until holds lead leftwards joining the corner at half height.

**15   One of These Days
Direct Finish 6a   ★★**
Do not traverse into the corner but continue direct.

16   The Famous Alto Sax Break NL 6c   ★
A very difficult climb up the blank wall to the right.

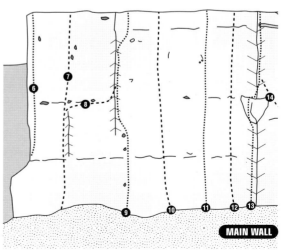

MAIN WALL

MAIN WALL

DATELINE WALL

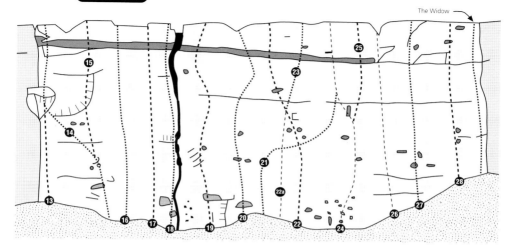

The Widow

17 Padarn Dance 6b ⭐
An eliminate. Climb the wall just to the left of Dateline. You must not touch this! Named after a legendary character, 'Tiger Mick' who would run through said Pub with a lighted newspaper thrust up his backside. Originally called 'Dance of the Flaming Arsehole!' Nice!

18 Dateline 5c ⭐⭐⭐
The obvious crack. A name chosen by the first ascentionist as climbing it made him late for a hot date. An E3 lead with good protection.

19 Sinbad 6b ⭐⭐
Start five feet right of Dateline at a very small arete. Climb the wall above moving almost into Dateline before wandering back right.

20 Depression 6b ⭐⭐
Make difficult moves past twin sloping pockets at ten feet and continue upwards.

21 Exit on Air 6b ⭐⭐⭐
Climb to a pebble band a few feet left of Black Magic and make a rising traverse across this to join Acid Test just below its crux. Finish up this route.

22 Black Magic 6a ⭐⭐⭐
A celebrated climb which is now a shadow of its former self thanks to an idiot with a big hammer and a small brain. The crux is low down and,

although the cement used to fill in the chipped holds alters this part of the route, it is still worth the effort. The Direct start (22a) is 6b.

23 Black Magic Direct Finish 6c ⭐
A difficult rightwards finish.

24 Acid Test 6a+ ⭐⭐
Begin below an old bolt and climb up to a prominent slot; traverse left for a few feet and finish direct. Has been led using a friend in the slot

25 Parker's Mood 6b
A direct finish to Acid Test.

26 Euphoria 6b
A difficult line a few feet to the right of Acid Test.

27 Never Mind the Acid 5c ⭐
Climb the wall 10ft left of the corner, trending right at the top to finish via an obvious crack.

28 Treadmill 5c
Climb the wall directly 5ft left of the corner.

The low traverse from Dateline into the corner is a popular and fingery 5c. Quitting just before The Widow is 5b. Coming into the traverse from the corner of One of These Days is more difficult and sustained, award yourself 6a (i.e. Limestone 6b)!

DATELINE WALL

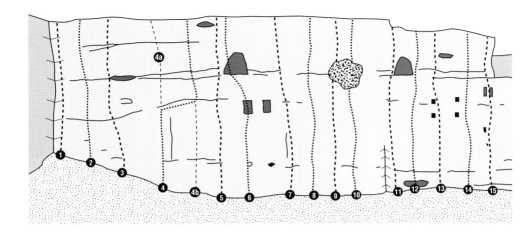

1   The Widow 5b
Climbs the short strenuous corner, often wet always dirty.

2   Jota 6a
Climb the wall 5 feet right of the corner.

3   Polar Bear 6b   **★★**
From a ledge five feet right of the corner make a very hard move to an obvious large horizontal pocket and continue above.

4   Time Passage 6b   **★**
To the right of the previous route climb the vague arete to an obvious break then traverse right for five feet and make easier moves up the wall above. There is a direct start at 6a (no.4b) and a direct finish at 6c (no.4a).

5   Cyclops 5b
Climb the wall just left of the two eyes.

6   Two Eyes 4c   **★★**
Climb up to the the large twin pockets and on through a scoop to finish.

7   Cornea 5c   **★★**
The wall just right of the two eyes.

8   Willy Simm's Silly Whim 6b
More of a boulder problem than a route, climb the wall using the vague layaway for your right hand and continue above.

9   Retina 5b   **★**
Below and left of the oak tree, climb direct to the top.

10 Nameless 4c
Climb the wall directly right of the oak tree.

11 Eliminate 4b
Climb the shallow corner moving slightly left at the break.

12 Goliath 5c   **★**
Climb the wall just right of the corner making a difficult move from the pockets to the large break.

13 Square Four 4b   **★**
Start below the four holds and climb direct. Try this one without the boreholes at 6a.

14 Greeting 5b
Climb the wall three feet right using a large pocket a few feet below the top.

PISA WALL

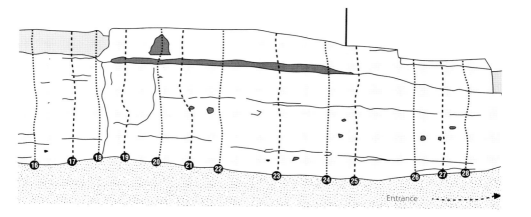

15 Handshake 5a　　　　　　　　　　★
Climb direct to shake hands with the twin slits near the top.

16 Pisa Wall 4a　　　　　　　　　　★★
Takes the leaning wall left of Straight Crack.

17 Warm Up 5b
Wall between Pisa Wall and Straight Crack.

18 Straight Crack 3c　　　　　　　★★
Climb the classic crack.

19 Eliminate Wall 5c
The wall between the two cracks without using them.

20 Mankey Road 5b　　　　　　　★★
The right hand crack. Feels harder becuase of its committing nature.

21 Monkey Grip 5a　　　　　　　　　★

22 Green Streaks 5b　　　　　　　　★
Climb the wall with the green streak running down it.

23 Fingers 5c
Climb the wall a few feet to the right.

24 Bushy Tale 5b　　　　　　　　　★
Climb the wall behind the tree directly to the top.

25 One Move 5c　　　　　　　　　　★
Climb the wall below the railing.
A traditional 5c!

26 Thumb Screw 6a
Use a poor bore hole to leave the ground. The second Thumb Screw at Pex.

27 Commando 6a
6 feet left of the arete. After the break the top is reached by using a sharp elongated fingerhold for the left hand.

28 Gorilla 5c　　　　　　　　　　　★
Left of the arete with a long move to finish.

Traverses: A wall with many traverses; the classic is 5c. Find the easiest way across from Gorilla to Two Eyes. The crux is reaching this route with your feet in the break. The rest you can discover for yourself.

The Grand Tour 1000ft 3a to 6c　★★★
The girdle traverse of Pex Hill is a fine achievement, make it as easy or as difficult, as high or low as you like.

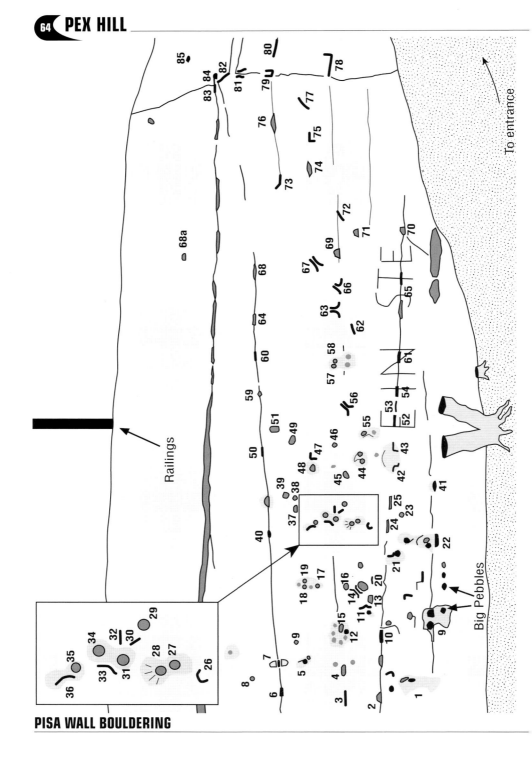

PISA WALL BOULDERING

"One of the best bouldering areas in the country". The Crag Guide to England and Wales.

We tried to create the worlds most complicated bouldering diagram, we think we may have succeeded. In years to come an Open University course will be available for the sole purpose of trying to find out what it all means. There are just too many holds which have been touched by the boulderers fingers! The selection of problems below is only the tip of the iceberg, space has been left for you to devise your own testpieces of the future. Whilst not being steep the problems below require great finger strength and good footwork if success is to be achieved.

1 6c V8
(22) 20, 14, 3, 6, break

2 Dyno 6c V9
(3) break

3 6c V7
(1) 20, 16, 36, 48 share, 50, break

4 Vitalite 6c V8
(22a) 12, 19, 18, break

5 Silly Boy 5c V3
(10) 17, 19, 40, break or miss out 40 at V5

6 Big Nick 6b V5
(1) 20, 18, 32, 35, 50, break

7 6b V4
(22, 41) 32, 30, 14, 19, 9, 8, break

8 5c V3
(25) 48, 50, break

9 Little Nick 6c V8
(52, 53) 46, 50, break

10 6a V4
(55, 31) 50, break

11 5c V3
(61) 31, 62, 60, break

12 Punks at Pex 6b+ V6+
(61, 62) 58, break

13 The Shot Hole 6b V4
(23) 58, 62 64, break

14 6b V7
(54, 61) 58, 69, 71, 74, 76, 81, 83, 85, top

15 The South West Overhang 6c V8
(66, 67) 64, break

16 Trad Sit Down 5c V1
(70) 71, 68, break

17 North West Sit Down 7a V10
(70) 72, 73, 68, break, 68a, top.

18 North West Overhang 6c V8
(72, 73) 68, break, 68a, top.

19 6c V6
(78) 75, 81, 83, 85, top.

20 The Pit Bull 6a V3
(78) 80, 81, 83, 85, top.

Traverses

21 Wild Horses 6c V9
(10) 20, 28, 32, 55, 46, 31, 58, 63, 64, 68, break to the right of 23.

22 Wild Horses Extension 6c V10
Share on 68, 68a, finish with left hand on top.

23 The Pit Bull Traverse 6b V8
Do not use break for feet (9) 22, share, 41, 42, 43, 54, 65, 69, 74, 76, 81, 83, 85, top

24 Shothole Traverse 6a+ V5
(42, 43) 61, 58, 69, 74, 76, 82, 83, 85, top.

New Problems

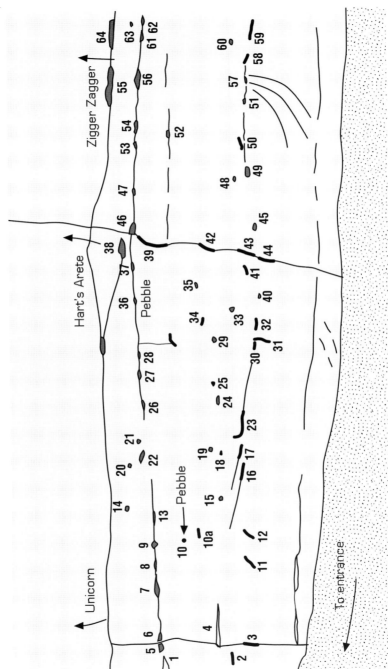

HART'S ARETE BOULDERING

Situated below Unicorn, Hart's Arete and Zigger Zagger the problems finish at an obvious break at 12 feet.

1 4b
(2) 1, break.

2 6a V1
(3) 5, 6, break.

3 The Mantle 6a V1
(4) break.

4 4c
4, 7, break.

5 5c V1
(11, 12) 10, 8, break. (not using the low break for the feet increases the grade to 6b V4.

6 The Denominator 6b+ V7
(11, 12) 10a, top break, no breaks for feet.

7 5c V1
(12, 15) 9, 14, break.

8 5c V1
(16, 17) 15, 13, break.

9 6c V7
(17), 19, 21, 20, break.

10 5b
(23), 18, 26, break.

11 5a
(23), 24, 26, 27, break.

12 6b V4
(30, 32), 25, 28, 27, break.

13 5b
(29), 28, break.

14 6a V2
(30, 32), 33, 29, break.

15 6c V9
(33), 35, 34, 36, break.

16 Hart's Arete 6a V2
Up the obvious arete, and onwards to the top! A harder version, 6b V4, laybacks just the arete to gain hold 37.

17 6b+ V6
(45), 47.

18 5b
(49), 48, 52, 54.

19 6a V2
(50, 51), 54.

20 5c V1
(51, 57), 54, 55.

21 5c V1
(58, 59), 60, 61, 62, 64.

Traverses

22 Grand Horizontal 6c V9+
(4), 11, 12, 16, 17, 23, 30, 31, 32, 33, 40, 41, 44. An even harder version continues into the corner of The Web.

23 Hart's Arete Traverse 6a V2
(1), 5, 6, 7, 8, 9, 13, 26, 27, 28, 36, 37, 46, 47, 53, 54, 56, 64

New Problems

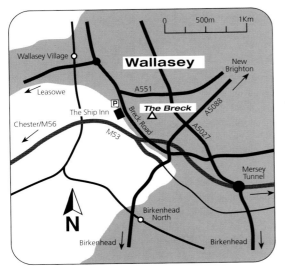

However enlightened the descriptions of The Breck may seem, one cannot escape the fact that it's a scruffy, graffiti ridden, dump; but the bouldering makes up for this. It's like finding a fiver in a pile of dung; you want it but will you pick it up?
Steve Bromley, a local climber.

GENERAL

The last word in urban crags. It's got the lot; rock blackened with industrial grime, Dickensian urchins, graffiti, dog dirt and the occasional broken bottle. Oh yeah, it's also got great bouldering and micro-routes. So do not be put off from visiting by my description exaggerating the worst, it is actually a nice place to climb and it will help you develop very strong fingers. It has produced a few world class climbers; OK so most of them buggered off to better places once they had become stars but this is where it all began.

ASPECT

There are four areas; the unusual Granny rock, the Bluebell Wall, Overhanging Wall and Who Wall. In my opinion the Bluebell Wall offers the best climbing with many routes and an infinite number of desperate problems which I have left to the visitor to discover.

APPROACH

The crags lie above Breck Road near the village of Wallasey on the B5145. When approaching from Liverpool turn right on leaving the Wallasey Tunnel (heading for New Brighton A5047) and turn left at the first set of lights on to Poulton Road. Continue over the motorway and the crag lies behind The Ship Inn. The quarry is not visible from the road but lies just to the right of the pub. Approach by an obvious path or drive round the back and enter via Millthwaite Road.

Bluebell Wall

The long wall with gardens at the top provides an array of fingery problems. People have been known to come here and never get off the ground (some of them now run climbing shops or edit climbing magazines!) The wall tends to seep in winter although the traverse usually stays dry.

1   **5a**   *
    Up and over the bulge.

2   **5a**   *
    Obvious crack.

3   **5c**   *
    From 2 small pockets to nice deep bi-doigts followed by long reaches and shoddy footholds to the top.

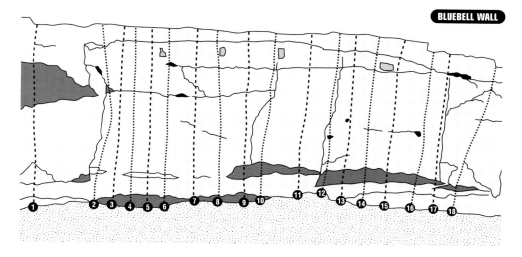

4 5a

5 5c ⋆⋆
Large 'sad looking' Hueco to crimpy break followed by a long move to the top break.

6 5c+
2 monos (one inside a pocket) lead to crimpy moves and a gripping reach to finish.

7 5b+

8 6a ⋆
Starting with your left hand in the pocket gain a flake via some awesome moves, then climb direct, avoiding the ledges.

9 6b+
Use the small mono next to the V slot then make crimpy, reachy moves up the wall.

10 6a ⋆⋆⋆
Faint lightning crack, technical and gripping.

11 5c

12 5c+ ⋆
The crack has a powerful start.

13 5b ⋆⋆
The diagonal shotholes. A brilliant problem with two unique 'cement' holds!

14 6a ⋆
Start on the big undercut climb directly passing two pockets and a letterbox slot on the way.

15 6a
From the large pocket reach through to the 'eyes' above.

16 5c
Undercut the big pocket to the right.

17 5c ⋆⋆
The crack; doesn't look much, does it?

18 5b
Up to the rickety tree root; use it as a way down.

Traverses
There are three traverses across the wall.
The best across the centre of the wall from route 2 to 16 is The Bluebell Traverse, an excellent 6a.
The top break is 5b, while along the bottom bulge is 5c.

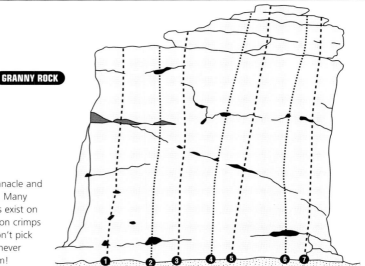

GRANNY ROCK

Granny Rock
The obvious isolated pinnacle and the first rock to dry out. Many problems and eliminates exist on the steeper side mainly on crimps and sloping pockets. Don't pick up cheater stones, you never know what's under them!

1 4b
Easy sloping pockets near left arete.

2 5a/5c
Use the crimp (easy) or the sandy pocket (hard).

3 5b   ******
Direct through big ledges.

4 5c   *****
Use 2 crimps in the diagonal, then the angled pocket to a big ledge. Good moves follow to the next break.

5 5c
From big diagonal ledges ascend direct.

6 6b+   *****
Undercut a 2 finger pocket to reach break, then finish tenuously.

7 Phil's Route 6a   ******
Reach to a 2 finger crimp with right hand and pull!
Many variations exist on the front of Granny, good training for the Alps!

Traverses
The following traverses are possible, do all four for a monster pump!

1 6b
Ground level from L to R under cracks to join 3.

2 Greg's Traverse 7a
Same again but keep under diagonal crack all the way.

3 Diagonal Crack 6a

4 Horizontal 5b

Who Wall
Named after the graffiti which once adorned it. It is definitely not Nirvana as the new graffiti suggests. A good place for beginners.

1 4c
Left arete.

2 5a
Wall above big pocket.

3 4c
Right trending overlap.

4 6a
Central wall on small pockets.

5 4b
Blunt rib on jugs.

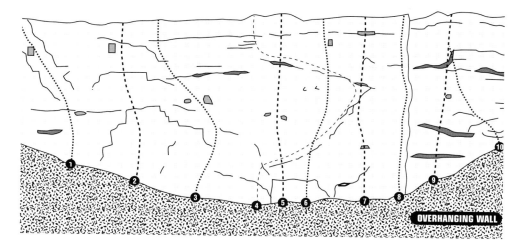

OVERHANGING WALL

6 6a/b
Mossy wall, scary!

7 5a
Right arete; hard start then jugs.

8 4b ∗
Wall around the corner on big ledges.

9 5c ∗
Boiler plate slab.
The traverse around this section is 4c.

Overhanging Wall
The largest wall at The Breck. A bit greasy, in winter the wall comes into condition when the canopy of leaves recedes. All the routes are hard so either go to the gym before you come here or set up your Bachar ladder on the toproping bolts.

1 Tom's Route 6b

2 Fighting Tans 6b

3 Woman's Weekly 6b

4 In The Jungle 6b ∗
Follow right-trending ledge system to join left-trending crackline at the top.

5 Overhanging Wall Direct 6c
From the Fireplace reach to a slanting ledge. Flakes out left lead to two large pockets and an awesome final move on crimps.

6 Pilli Winks 7a (F8a)
Shoddy holds lead up to a ledge from which a powerful slap off a flake gains a diagonal line of crimps leading to the top.

7 In The Jungle Direct 6c (F7b+) ∗∗
Use the kidney shaped pocket to gain the ledge, jump to the jugs then make a powerful mono move to the top. The best route on Merseyside according to one local!

8 Greasy Cobweb Crack 5c
Gnarly thin moves to ledges, oddly unlike crack climbing.

9 Flash In The Pan 6b
The wall right of the crack is grotty and fragile.

10 Unknown 5c
The wall further right, joining 9 at the overlap.

Traverses
The Breakfast Line is the low level traverse from 1 to 4, a sustained 7a

OVERHANGING WALL

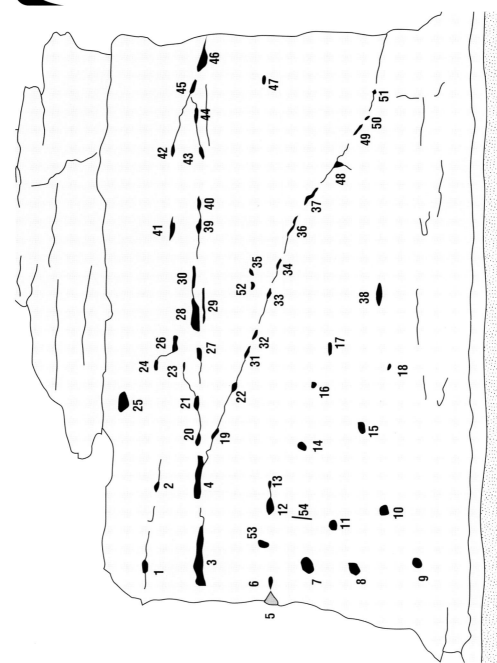

Bouldering on the Granny Rock

Diminutive but charismatic. Like Dudley Moore(?)

1 5b V1
Layback left arete without using the pockets or ledges.

2 6b V5
(10) 11, 12, 3, top.

3 6b+ V6
(12,13) top.

4 6a V3
(17) 52, 29, top.

5 5c V2
(15,14) 19, 21, 26, 24, top.

6 6b V5
(15) 13, 19, 2, top.

7 6b V5
(16,17) 32, 29, 41, break.

8 Brundlefly (Project)
(17,38) 29, 26, 24, break.

9 Old Shep 6b V5
(38) 17, 33, 29, 26, 24, break.

10 6b V5
(38) 17, 35, 29, 26, 24, break.

11 6b V5
(38) 36, 29, 26, 24, break.

12 6a V3
(936,37) 38, 40, 41, break.

13 5c V2
(36) 35, 29, 26, 24, break.

14 6a V2
(48) 44, traverse off.

15 Phil's Route 6a V3
(48,
51) 47, 44, any holds to the top.

16 6a+ V4
(37) 43, top.

17 'V' Poor! 7a V10
(53,54) 3, 2, 25.

18 6b V4
(33,34) 39, traverse right to arete and up.

19 6c V8
(38) 35, 23, 25, Top.

Traverse Problems

1 5b V1
The obvious break at 10 feet.

2 5c V3
The right to left rising traverse line, used for training before the first ascent of Positron, Gogarth. Just using the crack is 6a.

3 Geg's Traverse 7a V10
Under the 5c traverse to the left arete.

New Problems

GRANNY ROCK BOULDERING

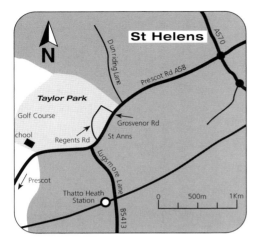

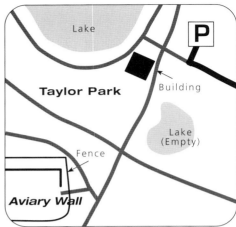

GENERAL

A recently developed quarry which has seen occasional toproping and bouldering over the years. It has now been extensively bolted and the climbing is very similar to Pex Hill. Remnants of the aviary that have given rise to many bird route names can be seen at the base of the wall.

ASPECT

The main walls can often remain damp after rain but it is a very pleasant summer venue, receiving the sun in the late afternoon. A couple of problems exist; firstly it seems like some of the local adolescents who hang out in the park love the sound of breaking glass. This has left quite a lot of the stuff at the base of the routes and the occasional missile has been known to fly. So let's be careful out there! **Secondly, the authorisation of access is not too clear and therefore a low profile is advised.**

APPROACH

The park lies off the A58 which runs between Prescot and St Helens. When travelling from Prescot take a left into Grosvenor Road shortly after The Grange Pub. When travelling from St Helens, Grosvenor Road is on the right shortly after the quaintly named "Bird ith' Hand" pub.

Park at the end of Grosvenor Road or follow signs into the park where there is a small car park. Walk into the park and veer left, skirting the lake on the higher path, past a lakeside building and straight over a crossroads in the path. The quarry entrance is down a sunken driveway ahead.

1   **Stop the Pigeon E1 5b**
A short route with the the crux at the top.

2   **The Dove From Above E3 6a**
A more sustained route with a nasty finish.

3   **Emu E4 6b**
Clip a bolt on the last route halfway up.

4   **Shitehawk E3 6a**
With traffic it will become a decent route.

5   **Heckle and Jeckyll E3 5c**
Gain the pod from the right, then make nice moves directly up the wall.

6   **Stone the Crows E4 6b**
Follow the right hand start of the last route but break out right before the big pocket and finish directly up the wall.

TAYLOR PARK INTRODUCTION

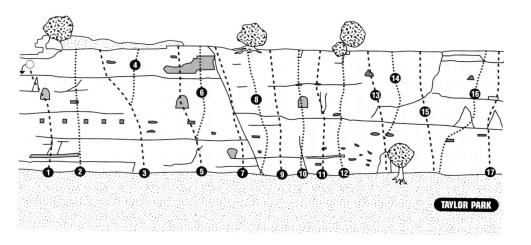

7 Aviary Crack E2 5b *

The diagonal crack.

8 Daffy Duck E3 5c

Nice climbing up the wall to the right.

9 Roadrunner E3 6a

Another good route with some fingery climbing.

10 Tweety Pie E4 6a **

Climb directly to the big hole ('Tweety's Cage')
and exit up the wall above with difficulty.

11 Foghorn Leghorn E4 6a

A similar line into the long slot to the right with
the crux at the top.

12 Hawkeye E4 6b **

A difficult crimpy route up the blank wall to the
right.

13 Birdman E4 6a

Climb out of the damp recess and head for the
big pocket high on the wall.

14 Phoenix E4 6b *

Climb the last route to the second bolt, then
move right to a good finish on the headwall.

15 Maltese Falcon E4 6a **

16 Cuckoo's Nest E3 5c *

A good route; finish just right of the oak tree.

17 Dead Parrot E3 5c

18 Aviary Corner E1 5b

Climb the obvious corner. There is only one bolt
at half height.

There is a traverse across the wall at a low level,
from 1-12 it is 5c, from 13-18 it's 5b; the two
have yet to be linked. There are some chipped
looking holds on the steep wall to the right of
the corner. Right again there are three Eco-Bolts;
why?

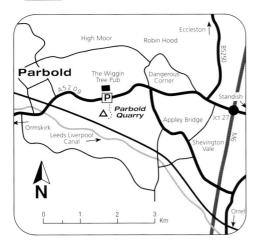

GENERAL

Upon initial inspection it would seem Parbold is almost as bad as some of the things people climb on in the South West! However some of the climbs are quite good and deserve more attention, which would raise the status of the venue to that of a typical small crag in the peak district. Honest!

APPROACH

The quarry is situated a short distance from the top of Parbold Hill. There is car parking in a lay-by/view point opposite the Wiggin Tree pub at the top of the hill on the A5209, 2Km from Parbold and two and a quarter miles from the Standish exit on the M6 (junction 27). From the lay-by take the path which runs down the side of a landfill site to a stile at the bottom. Turn right and follow the wall and fence round to another stile at the bottom right corner of the field. Continue along the path over this stile and the next one, then enter the quarry by a path on the right.

ASPECT

The quarry is mostly filled with trees and is between 35-50ft in height. For the most part it is solid, but in parts, especially around Wiggin, the tops are treacherous. The routes are described from left to right, starting from an earthy corner at the top end of the quarry. The numbers painted on the rock do **not** refer to the routes as they appear in this guide.

Main Face

This is the first section of climbable rock right of the earthy corner.

1   Wiggin S 4b

From the earthy corner follow an easy line of flaky ledges diagonally right and finish up a short corner. Loose.

2   Soft Joe VS 4c

A direct line that finishes up the final corner of Wiggin.

3   Grouse Beaters HVS

Start 4ft further right and climb the cracks directly through the overhangs, step left at the tree.

4   Stingy Mudpuppy VS 4c

The obvious flake crack 15ft right of the earthy corner. The finish seems to have collapsed! Best avoided!

5   Please Allow Me To Introduce Myself VS 5a

Gain the hanging crack to the right and follow it to a loose finish; then climb the pocketed green slab to a tree belay.

6   Section 47 HVS 5a

Start behind the large tree which grows near the foot of the crag and climb the wall via a vague crack; there may be a peg runner at 30ft!

7   Too Loud a Solitude E5 6a

Start 15ft left of 'The Crack' beneath an overlap and slightly overhanging groove at an obvious ledge. Climb up to the undercut on the right of the scoop, make a long move to pass the overlap then finish rightwards up the choss.

8   The Crack HVS 5a

Start 16ft right at the top of a small mound and climb the obvious deep crack via a sentry box, which is awkward to enter. Finish on the left.

9   Marble Gorge VS 4b

Climb the wall to the right to a shallow scoop, then step up and left to a ledge and move left again to finish up The Crack.

10 The Bull 11m HS 4b

Take a direct line past a giant ring peg to a finish on the right of the top neb. Borehole runner near top.

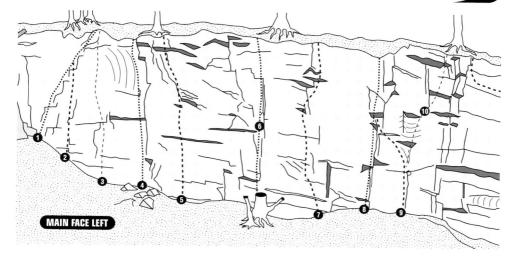

MAIN FACE LEFT

11 Vishnu Temple 11m VS 4c
From the point where the ground level drops slightly, climb up to the overhangs, and attain a standing position on an obvious small neb. Reach the ledge above and finish as for Neglect.

12 Original Route VD
Start about 3 metres right and climb up and right to a large ledge at 16ft, traverse right for 5 metres to another ledge and finish rightwards.

13 Neglect VD
Climb up to the right side of the large ledge on Original Route, then move left and up to the top via an obvious series of ledges.

14 Bird Lime VS 4c
A direct line to the top via a series of bore marks.

15 Sacrificial Block S 4b
Start by an iron spike in the ground and climb the wall to a projecting ledge on the right at 30ft (there is a slightly harder line a metre right). From the ledge climb diagonally right to the top.

16 Phantom Ranch VS 4c   *
Start a metre right and climb up and right to an overhang at 15ft. Surmount this with difficulty and continue up the wall above to the top.

17 Fossil Overhang HS 4a   *
Start behind the tree 4ft left of the right arete. Climb up to an iron spike above the overhang, then continue just left of the arete until the arete can be joined for the last move.

18 Lumberjack Ridge VD   *
The arete which bounds the Main Wall on its right.

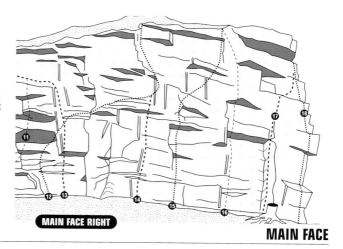

MAIN FACE RIGHT

MAIN FACE

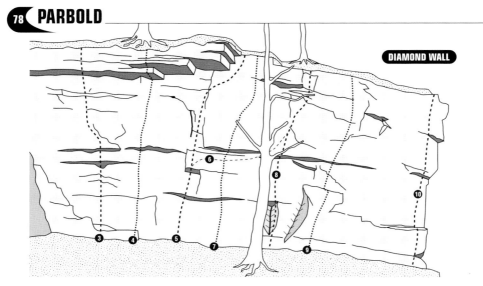

DIAMOND WALL

On the wall at right angles to the Main Wall are two further climbs not shown on the diagram.

1   Rolthinux VD
Start a 4ft of the arete behind a tree and follow an obvious diagonal line to the top.

2   Lucky Grab HS 4b
The blunt arete 13ft further right, then the wall above to a tree.

Diamond Wall
This is the next wall which faces the same direction as Main Wall.

3   Lost in Space 2 5c
On the left hand side is a small crack which is followed to ledges and a finish over the roof.

4   Spaced Cadet E3 5c
Start 10ft right of the previous route with a boulder problem start and RP protection for the moves over the roof.

5   Conquistador Aisle E1 5b
Start below the right end of the large top overhang and follow a direct line to the top.

6   Kamikaze Cuckoo VS 4c
Climb the previous route to the horizontal break,

then hand traverse right and finish up Gillen's Route.

7   Kam VS 5a
Start nearly 7ft right and make a long reach for a ledge. Then continue to a break finishing up the wall to the left of the overhang on Gillen's Route.

8   Gillen's Route HS 4a   *
Climb to the halfway ledge via a small sentry box, then step left and continue up to an overhang, which can be passed on its right.

9   Little Wall Climb VD
Gain the anvil a metre right and continue to the top by a right-leading line.

10 Right Hand Edge Route HS 4a   **
The right arete of Diamond Wall.

End Bay
The remainder of the quarry is known as the End Bay. Sometimes part of this can be flooded, which obviously gives its own problems.

11 A Worthwhile Pastime - But a Sad Ambition E5 6c   *
The wall of the old aid route Ball Strangler (A2!) provides a steep and sustained testpiece. Starting at a flat hold on the arete move right to gain a bendy peg then up to reach a break. A long

DIAMOND WALL

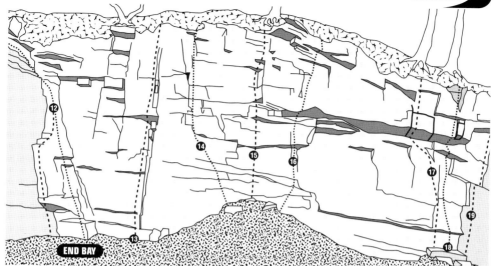

reach right to a triangular notch is followed by a couple of more difficult moves up the arete to finish.

12 Lucky Strike VS 4b
The corner on the right is climbed direct, or via a nose on the left. Exit left at the top.

13 Lava Falls E2 5c
The blocky overhanging crack 13ft right of the left corner of the bay.

14 Pit Fundamentalist   F7b+ E6 6b   *
A bolted line up the steep wall between Lava Falls and Desolation Row. Bouldery moves lead to a big horizontal break; more difficult moves above allow one to reach a short vertical crack and triangular notch. Move rightwards up the wall above. Don't touch the routes on either side!

15 Desolation Row E2 5c   *
Start below the large tree in the centre of the back wall of the bay and climb direct up the leaning wall. Has sprouted a couple of bolts.

16 Really Free E2 5b
The hanging crack on the right has also sprouted bolts.

17 Reach for the Sky E2 5b
The bulging wall 10ft left of Poverty, Poverty. Traverse left to a crack and then climb the roof above.

18 327 HVS 5b
From just over a 4ft left of Poverty, Poverty, take the overhangs directly below a large oak. Loose high up.

19 Poverty, Poverty HVS 5a
The right corner of the bay, with a difficult move onto a ledge on the right at two-thirds height.

20 Hammock A2
The thin crack that splits the final wall from right to left, finishing past a small tree.

21 Dick Dastardly and Muttley E1 5c
A free version of Vulcan's Forge. Start as for Hammock and follow the thin crack which leads more directly to the top.

22 Evening Crack HS 4b
The thin crack on the right of the final wall.

23 Grassy Overhangs V Diff
Start a 4ft right and climb up and right over overhangs to the top.

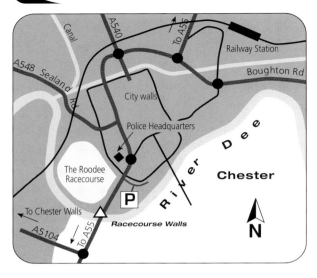

"There was a constant battle between trying to get fit and the temptations of the good life. Al (Rouse) started training again, particularly on the Chester Racecourse Walls, and became very fit".Brian Hall in **Alan Rouse, A Mountaineer's Life.**

GENERAL

The supporting walls of the Grosvenor Bridge in Chester have been used for some time by local climbers; however, it must be stressed that the reporting of such activities in this book is in no way an indication of a right to climb. This magnificent bridge which spans the River Dee was designed by Thomas Harrison (1744-1829) and when it was opened in October 1832 by Princess Victoria it had the largest single span in the world at 200 feet.

The first recorded climb was in 1832 by Princess Victoria who climbed the stunning arete in formal dress and tiara before an adoring crowd, a fine effort which was years ahead of its time. Since then local climbers have used these man-made walls for training, traversing backwards and forwards like nodding dogs.

APPROACH

The walls lie below the A483 which runs from Chester to North Wales. They are next to the River Dee on the city side below the Grosevenor Bridge. They are known as the Racecourse Walls as they are situated next to the ancient Roodee racetrack; another useful

landmark is Chester Castle which overlooks the bridge. There is a pay and display car park opposite the castle which gives easy access to the walls.

ASPECT

The rock is sandstone shaped into large blocks which have not been finished too precisely, thereby leaving 'natural' holds.The walls reach up to 35ft in height, receive the afternoon and evening sun and provide crag adventure in a city setting. Wine bars, cinemas and restuarants are never far away. They tend to stay dry in poor weather and when occasionally they do get wet they are quick to dry. However, there is one problem, the rat population!

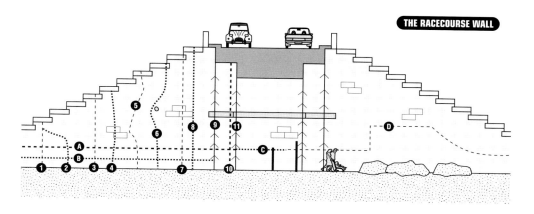

THE RACECOURSE WALL

A visit here may afford the only chance a mortal has of doing all of these famous routes in a single day!

1 A Separate Reality 5c
The name says it all!

2 Left Wall 5c
Climb the stunning left wall to a leftwards traverse near the top.

3 Footless Crow 6a
A modern classic.

4 Wall Of Horrors 6a
The first ascentionist could only hang on the crux holds for 50 minutes before fatigue took over.

5 Salathe Wall 6a+
Now free.

6 Right Wall 5c
Through the small port hole.

7 Chouca 6a
A difficult start on pockets.

8 Genesis 6a
The impressive wall at its highest, a bold solo!

10 The Naked Edge 6a
The big arete "More gripping than soloing Right Wall." Phil Davidson after an on-sight solo ascent.

11 The Corner 5a
Bridging below the bridge. Climb as high as you dare.

12 Archangel 5c
Another fine arete.

Traverses
From just left of A Seperate Reality to a railing underneath the arch the wall can be traversed at two heights. The higher more obvious line (A) is 5c. The lowest is 6c (B), the continuation (C) is 5c+. If you link both the traverses climbing above the metal spikes and barbed wire of the fence award yourself E6 6a! The opposite wall of the arch provides another 6a traverse. The second wall on the car park side is traversed at a grade of 6a. Another long traverse, 5b, lies on the walls overlooking the race-course below and to the left of the descent steps.

Other Crags

Anglican Cathedral Quarry

In the grounds of the magnificent cathedral on Hope Street in Liverpool city centre is a graveyard with quarried walls. Fall off and eliminate the undertakers!

Beeston Castle

A fine-looking sandstone outcrop. Many people have climbed routes here in the past, including the authors. The black walls and overhangs below the castle are bigger than anything else in Cheshire. However our land is looked after by the Department of the Environment who in their infinite wisdom have decided that climbing is forbidden.

Irby Quarry

Situated near the crossroads at Irby Hill, south of the village of Frankby. This quarry offers several routes in the Diff to Severe range.

Manley Knoll

A small outcrop situated at Manley Village near Delamere Forest in Cheshire. Some small routes and worthwhile boulder problems can be contrived. It lies on private land.

Thurstaston Hill

A small sandstone quarry near Thurstaston village on the Wirral.

Whiston Quarry

Situated behind the Nurses' Home at Whiston Hostpital, Merseyside. Has one of the most impressive walls of overhanging sandstone on Merseyside. Unfortunatley no climbing is allowed and it is expected to be filled in with waste in the near future.

Woolton Quarry

A big sandstone quarry in Woolton Village, Liverpool. This quarry has seen climbing in the past but now has houses standing in it. You will have to buy one to climb.

Pumping Station outside Frodsham

A small square cut quarry just off the Delemere road on the outskirts of Frodsham. Owned by North West Water and used as a pumping station. Access is unclear. All the cracks and aretes in the quarry have been climbed; the big diagonal one at the back of the quarry is the best. The blank walls would provide some difficult climbing although the steep vegetation at the top of the cliff presents a serious hazard.

Other possibilities exist for climbing in old railway cuttings across the region, along the banks of the canal in the centre of Chester and on various buildings and bridges. A visit to your local climbing wall may be more productive however!

Beer and Victuals

Helsby and Frodsham

Both villages contain many good pubs. Try The Netherton Hall located just outside Frodsham on the Helsby road, with real ale and very good food, while The Helter Skelter in Frodsham offers many fine ales and good meals. There are also a couple of good fish and chip shops and cafes in Frodsham.

Frogsmouth

The Travellers Rest pub sits to the right of the car park and is the usual post climbing venue. Runcorn has many cafes and pubs; none are worthy of merit.

Pex Hill

The village of Cronton has two very welcoming pubs, The Black Horse and The Unicorn situated at the cross roads at the centre of the village; both serve food. Cronton also has a very fine fish and chip shop.

The Breck

The Ship, located on Breck Road within sight of the quarry is the traditional apres-climb meeting place. However, for a great pub try The Stanley Cask on Rake Lane, New Brighton for good food and real ale.

Taylor Park

A few hundred yards from the park on the main drag is the imposing Bird ith' Hand. Soft drinks and tea can be purchased in the park during the summer months.

Night Clubs

Be very careful when visiting late venues in Widnes, St Helens and Runcorn; many a pretty boy has lost his looks in these towns and has consequently been reduced to pursuing a career in Rugby League. You have been warned. Liverpool however has one of the most relaxed licensing policies in the country; if you can't enjoy a night out in this city you must be dead! There are many good pubs: The Philharmonic (traditional) on Hope Street, The Everyman Bistro (real ale and food) also on Hope Street, The Modo (trendy) on Wood Street and any pub in Matthew Street (bawdy!). The inquistive amongst you may find Hitler's auntie's pub, where he stayed as a young man before the second world war. World famous clubs to visit are Cream, Voodoo and Garlands, who recentley hosted a night called fairies across the Mersey! Enough said. Grab a granny/grandaddy clubs exist everywhere. Have fun!

Climbing Clubs

The following contact addresses will change over time, if in doubt contact tne BMC.

Acme Walkers
14 Bramhall, Stockport, Cheshire.
Anabasis Mountaineering Club
9 Broxton Ave. Prenton, Birkenhead, Wirral, Merseyside.
Caper Montis Mountaineering Club
161 Harwood St., Darwen, Lancashire.
Chester Mountaineering Club
Nobby Wright, 101 Newhall Rd, Upton, Chester, Cheshire. 01244 314 276
Fylde Mountaineering Club
Frank Towne, 65 School Lane, Newton, Preston, Lancashire. 01253 779 471
Gwyder Mountain Club
23a Napps Way, Liverpool.
Innominata Mountain Club
Lady Barn House School, Schools Hill, Cheadle, Cheshire.
John Moores University Mountaineering Club
Students Union, Haigh Building, Maryland St. Liverpool.

Karabiner Mountaineering Club
23 Gerrard Ave. Timperley, Cheshire.
Lancashire Caving and Climbing Club
Sandra Hancock, 137 Dean Church Lane, Bolton Lancashire BL3 4EQ. 01204 63176
Lancashire Mountaineering Club
Bernard Smith, 10 Chesterbrook, Ribchester, Preston, Lancashire PR3 3XT. 01254 878 365
Liverpool Mountaineering Club
Allen Mc Donald, 32 Prentice Road, Rock Ferry, Wirral L42 4PP. 0151 645 3125
Manchester Metropolitan Mountaineering Club
15 Furness Road, Fallowfield, Manchester.
Manchester University Mountaineering Club
The Athletic Union, 333 Oxford Rd, Manchester.
Meseyside Fire Brigade Mountaineering Club
5 Robywell Way, Billinge, Lancashire.
Meseyside Mountaineering Club
Bill Sutherland, 46 Rimmer Ave. Liverpool 0151 489 5624.
Vagabond Mountaineering Club
Arthur Green, 26 Ballantrae Road, Allerton, Liverpool, L18 6JQ. 0151 724 3519

Climbing Shops

Cotswold	Manchester	0161 2364 123
Ellis Brighams	Liverpool	0151 709 6912
	Manchester	0161 833 0746
	Chester	01244 318 311
Nick Escourt	Altrincham	0161 928 6613
Tor	Widnes	0151 424 2225

There are also climbing shops at a number of climbing walls; see the directory for details.

Conservation and Wildlife

Sandstone crags and their immediate environment are fragile. Please respect the rock and surrounding landscape. Some of the crags in this guide receive a hammering throughout a climbing season and the last ten years in particular has seen erosion on an unprecedented scale. Please act with responsibility and challenge others who do not, or in the future we may be doomed to go indoors or travel great distances for a few hours' climbing.

Do: Take away rubbish
Do: Follow access agreements and respect seasonal restrictions
Do: Exercise restraint when cleaning the rock
Do Not: Abseil down established routes (or over the top at Frogsmouth)
Do Not: Chip or wire brush

Helsby and Frodsham

Frodsham crags situated on Woodhouse Hill are managed by the Woodland Trust and Helsby crag is managed by the National Trust both comprise steep sandstone escarpment surrounded by diverse mature woodland of oak, beech and birch.

This habitat supports a wide variety of birds, mammals and invertebrates as well as typical woodland flora. Birds include sparrowhawks, owls, jays, warblers, nuthatches, tree creepers and great spotted woodpeckers. Indeed Helsby crag offers evidence of the success of conservation policies in that peregrine falcons and ravens have recently bred there. Climbers are asked to be aware of voluntary nesting restrictions especially likely on Central Buttress.

Foxes, badgers, squirrels and bats are regularly seen close to the crags; once again the soft nature of the rock and the fragile nature of the vegetation and sandy soils lends itself easily to erosion and climbers are asked to keep to footpaths when approaching the crag and when descending from the top of the crag.

Pex Hill

Pex Hill is managed by the Knowsley Ranger Service under a Countryside Stewardship Agreement as a lowland heathland. The heathland is an unnatural habitat entirely created by man and certain species of invertebrate and birds have become dependent on heathland for survival.

The existing cover of bracken, gorse and heather surrounded by oak woodland provides valuable cover for a variety of wildlife. Typical birds include the common tits, blackcaps, goldcrests, yellow hammers and sparrowhawks. There is a great variety of butterflies in the summer months. In addition Pex is home to a colony of the rare common lizard.

The quarry has been designated a regionally important Geological and Geomorphical Site (RIGS) and both rangers and local climbers would ask you to respect this.
It is also important that any climbers who feel that they need to clean routes of heather and gorse etc. should consult the rangers first.

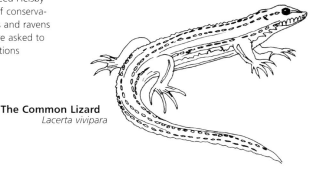

The Common Lizard
Lacerta vivipara

Frogsmouth

Frogsmouth is one of several quarries on Runcorn Hill designated a Local Nature Reserve principally because of its rare heathland habitat. The demise of quarrying left an acid soil perfect for the development of heathland and, as this largely grows on top of the quarry, climbers are requested to refrain from abseiling, topping out or sitting on the top and enjoying the views. This is one of the reasons the crag has developed as a sports climbing venue.

The Nuthatch
Sitta europea

The quarry is an important fossil site and dinosaur footprints have been discovered here. The sandstone face stretches along the length of one side of Happy Valley but climbing is restricted to certain parts of the crag (see guide). This is to limit the disturbance to plants and wildlife, namely little owls, bats and the only section of bilberry, a notable heathland plant, on Runcorn Hill.

The heathland and associated woodland is home to rare plants and animals like the above mentioned bilberry and the rare common lizard. Indeed it is one of the few areas locally where the equally rare hangdogger with its raucous cries and colourful plumage can be observed. In the surrounding woodlands greater spotted woodpeckers, sparrowhawks, jays, the common tit and various species of warbler may be found.

The Treecreeper
Certhia familiaris

The Goldcrest
Regulus regulus

CLIMBING WALLS

KEY Bouldering Leading Cellar/ board Shop Cafe

CHESTER

Northgate Arena
Victoria Street, Chester. CH2 2AU
01244 380 444

Chester Walls
Chester Bank Business Park, Riverside, Saltney, Clywd.
01244 682 626

ELLESMERE PORT

Epic Leisure Centre
McGarva Way, Ellesmere Port. L65 9HH
0151 355 6432

LIVERPOOL

Archbishop Beck School
Cedar Road, Aintree. L9 9AF
0151 525 6326

Note: School use only

The Climbing House
6 Lipton Close, Brasenose Ind Estate, Bootle. L20 8PU
0151 922 2999

Netherton Activity Centre
Glovers Lane, Netherton. L30 3TL
0151 525 5160

Prescot School
Knowsley Park Lane. L34 3NB
0151 426 5571

Rydal Youth Centre
384 Stanley Road, Kirkdale. L2
0151 922 4220

Vernon Sangster Sports Centre
Stanley Park, Priory Road, Anfield, Liverpool, L4 7XH
0151 260 6131

The Wade Smith Wall
Wade Smith Outdoor Athletics, Mathew Street. L1
0151 922 2999

SOUTHPORT

Southport YMCA
81 Houghton Street. PR9 0PR
01704 538 317

ST HELENS

St Helens YMCA
Nunn Street, St Helens. WA9 1SF
01744 25813

Tuition Available   Equipment Hire   Other Sports Facilities

WARRINGTON

North West Face
St Anns Church, Winwick Road, Warrington. WA2 7NE
01925 65002

Great Sankey Leisure Centre
Barrowhall Lane, Great Sankey. WA5 3AA
01925 724411

ORMSKIRK

Cliffs Barn
Woods Lane, Mawdesley, Lancashire. L40 2RL
01704 822 644

PRESTON

Preston
West View Liesure Centre, Ribbleton Lane, Preston.
01772 796 788

MANCHESTER

Armitage Sports Centre
Old Hall Lane, Manchester.
0161 740 1491

Broughton Recreation Centre
Camp Street, Salford. M7 9ZT
0161 792 2375

Abraham Moss Centre
Crescent Road, Crumpsall, Manchester.
0161 740 1491

McDougal Centre
University of Manchester, Oxford Road. M13 9PL
0161 275 4960

Members use only

Salford University
The Crescent, Salford, Manchester
0161 737 6206

MARPLE

Rope Race
Goyt Mill, Upper Hibbert Lane, Marple. SK6 7HX
0161 426 0226

GLOSSOP

Glossop Leisure Centre
High Street East, Glossop, Derbyshire. SK13 8PM
01457 863 223

ALTRINCHAM

Altrincham Sports Centre
Oakfield Road, Altrincham. WA15 8EW
0161 224 0404

Yorkshire
Gritsone
Bouldering

the definitive guide to the
best bouldering in Yorkshire
and one of the best areas
in the world!

by Alan Cameron-Duff

200 pages 20 areas
over 3000 problems
20 superb photographs

Available 30th September 1998
order direct from Stone
25 Burnley Rd East, Waterfoot,
Rossendale Lancs BB4 9AG
E-Mail stone@zen.co.uk